THE USE AND ABUSE OF OFFICE POLITICS

ABOUT THE AUTHOR

Mark started his working life in sales and marketing before studying and working in the area of social services. It was here that he gained his insight into dealing with people and came to understand the complexities of human behaviour. After a number of years involved in counselling and social work he decided to pursue a career in the corporate world, initially focusing on training and development, and later concentrating on organisational development and change.

Starting in the mid-1980s, Mark worked for a number of organisations in Human Resource and Organisational Development roles, which exposed him to a wide range of markets and cultures. During the last ten years he has worked predominately in the area of large scale organisational development and change.

In 1994 he founded his own consulting business, and is now Managing Director of Matrix Global, an organisation specialising in executive development and change management. Mark has worked with organisations such as News Limited, John Fairfax, ACP, Microsoft, Wang, Qantas, British Airways, SOCOG, Walt Disney, Woolworths and Big W.

Mark is based in Sydney, Australia and while he spends most of his time in Australia he is also in demand as an international keynote speaker and presenter.

Mark has qualifications in theology, counselling and psychotherapy as well as postgraduate qualifications in management, business, training and development management.

Chapter 1

POLITICS IN THE WORKPLACE

HOW IT ALL WORKS

There is no sea more dangerous than the ocean of practical politics—none in which there is more need of good pilotage and of a single, unfaltering purpose when the waves rise high.

Thomas Henry Huxley

'I am completely fed up with this situation. All I want to do is get on with what I'm paid to do—I don't want to be continually bogged down in all of the politics that goes on around this place. It saps up so much of my time and energy, I spend most of my day taking the daggers out of my back.'

Wouldn't you like a dollar for every time you have heard someone say something like that? Everyone at some stage in their working life has to cope with the political environment that exists within organisations. Research suggests that it is the political skills of an individual that are most influential in determining stagnation or promotion in their job, indicating that developing such skills is vital to career success (see Table 1). It is surprising how little attention people give to understanding this topic and to strategically creating for themselves a positive political environment that will enhance their career. *The Use and Abuse of Office Politics* is designed to help you negotiate your way through the minefield of organisational politics. It will assist you in understanding your political environment and help you develop a strategy for career progression, using this knowledge as leverage.

One of the challenges in addressing the topic of politics within organisations is that, by nature, the political issues that percolate, bubble and sometimes explode within organisations

1

are often subliminal or intangible—try to 'catch' a political situation or add some substance to the latest story surging through the office and you will often come up empty handed. It's like trying to bucket steam. Politics in organisations is a shadowland—it exists on the dark side of the moon. Few can really define it, even fewer will talk about it and no one in their right mind will ever admit to practising it. Despite the elusive nature of politics in the work environment, it is responsible for inefficiency and significant amounts of 'downtime', and on an individual level it is a major cause of stress and anxiety. Political conflict among employees at all levels reduces productivity, stifles innovation and creativity, decreases morale, hinders personal and business growth, undermines the quality of products and service to the customer. In the end, workplace politics can significantly affect your organisation's bottom line. Yet regardless of such disruption and negativity very little is said or done to minimise its effects.

People and politics

Politics is a phenomenon that exists wherever human beings interact, especially where they interact with the intention of achieving a common goal or sharing a mutual interest. Manoeuvring in political situations is a skill that is developed from the moment we realise it is possible for us to gain advantages by exhibiting certain behaviours and controlling circumstances. We compete for the attention of our parents; we take the teacher an apple; we pass on information about our siblings that puts them in a bad light but makes us look good . . . it all sounds like politics to me. Is it any wonder that when we arrive in the workforce we bring some of these characteristics with us?

Organisational politics isn't restricted to the business environment, of course. Just look at the political intrigue that is played out in church groups, at the golf club or in any other activity that involves people trying to organise themselves. It's a 'people' thing. People = politics = people is the simple

Table 1 Politics at work survey

	Strongly agree	Agree	Disagree	Strongly disagree	Unsure
Politics is a common phenomenon in most organisations	89.14	10.86	0	0	0
You have to be political to get ahead at work	34.78	50.0	15.21	0	0
Politics is exercised at all levels of the organisation	52.17	43.47	4.34	0	0
Politics in the workplace reduces efficiency	21.73	47.82	17.39	8.69	2.17
Politics is essential for organisations to operate	2.17	43.47	43.47	4.34	4.34
The higher you are in an organisation the more politics	45.62	32.6	19.56	2.17	0
Powerful executives don't need to use politics	2.17	8.69	45.65	43.47	0
Organisations should try to eliminate politics at work	15.21	32.6	36.95	10.86	4.34
Organisations without politics would be a happier place to work	28.26	39.13	34.78	2.17	10.86

equation. It springs from the basic human propensity to try to satisfy a wide range of psychological needs. We have a strong desire to control our own destinies and, wherever possible, we will try to influence the outcome of circumstances to our advantage. In theory, this puts us in a better position to ensure that either our base survival and security needs, or our more advanced psychological needs for prestige, autonomy or self-actualisation, are realised. Politics in these terms is an issue of personal interest and advantage and, because it is so closely associated with our instincts, it usually occurs at an unconscious level. Most of the time we aren't even aware it is happening. Consequently, when an individual or circumstance stands in the way of the satisfaction of our psychological needs, we will try to manoeuvre around, under, over or even through it to ensure that those needs are met. This ensuing situation is potentially political.

It is possible that some readers may feel a bit prickly about this rather simplistic explanation, but it is important to accept that these basic psychological drives are in themselves neither positive or negative. The telling factor that propels political behaviour in the workplace into the realms of moral or ethical issues is the balance of motives between personal and organisational goals. This balance is explored in more detail when we look at the two faces of politics at work—positive politics and negative politics.

Although it is emotionally and intellectually draining at times, there is no way of totally avoiding political environments that exist within organisations. If you choose to be successful in your career then, as someone once said, 'You've got to play to stay.' One person I interviewed about the importance of political savvy at work stated, 'I would like to think that it had nothing to do with it, that people were simply assessed on their competence and ability to do the job—but that wouldn't be living in the real world.' A journalist responding to a survey I conducted on the Internet pointed out that 'Every organisation has informal, political structures, to ignore them is career suicide. It's difficult to impress the boss if his secretary hates you'. Another respondent, operating in a line management position for a manufacturing organisation, put it this way: 'You constantly need to keep an ear to the ground to protect your interests. Otherwise you are going to get run over'.

Most people see politics at work as being negative and underhanded, yet they will usually acknowledge that it forms an essential part of organisational life and career success. Organisational politics does not have to be negative and destructive—it can be positive and constructive, working to the benefit of both individuals and organisations. This book is dedicated to helping you build the skills you need to exercise positive politics in your workplace and create for yourself an environment that will be a springboard to career success. Growing a positive political environment is a process, not an event. This chapter provides you with a practical model to help you implement this process.

Organisations are political webs

Organisations are often represented by neat and orderly charts depicting clear lines of authority and responsibility. When managers are asked to illustrate how the organisation is structured, most still drag out the familiar 'org chart' that depicts hierarchical reporting lines. These charts provide a very limited, one-dimensional image of the interactions that take place, generally focusing only on functional or operational aspects of the organisation.

Figure 1 Hierarchical relationships

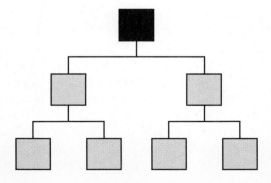

5

Hierarchical 'org charts' of the type illustrated in Figure 1 identify only the more formal aspects of organisations:

- where the authority lies—boss/subordinate relationships
- how and where decisions are made
- centres of control and position power
- cost points
- functional or operational responsibilities.

While we are all familiar with organisations depicted in this way, such representation is inadequate when trying to illustrate the complex networks of alliance, influence and power that eddy and swirl within and between these formal structures. When trying to explain the informal structures that exist within the work environment it is easier to think of them in terms of political webs that link individuals via sometimes strong, and at other times tenuous, strands—not just a single web but masses of interlinking and interrelated webs. The strands of these political webs represent relationships or associations that for one reason or another have been formed for mutual benefit. They become the basis of communication between individuals for negotiation, agreement and co-operation and are often the means for getting things done by sidestepping more formal channels.

Figure 2 Political webs

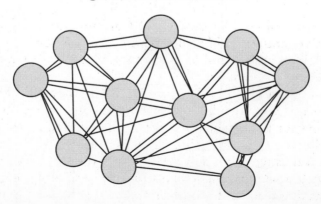

THE USE AND ABUSE OF OFFICE POLITICS

HOW TO SURVIVE AND THRIVE IN THE CORPORATE JUNGLE

MARK HOLDEN

ALLEN&UNWIN

For Benny and Cilla, and all of my friends who enrich my journey

First published in 1998 by Business and Professional Publishing
This edition first published in 2003 by Allen & Unwin
83 Alexander Street
Crows Nest NSW 2065
Australia
Phone: (61 2) 8425 0100
Fax: (61 2) 9906 2218
Email: info@allenandunwin.com
Web: www.allenandunwin.com

National Library of Australia
Cataloguing-in-Publication entry:

Holden, Mark, 1957– .
The use and abuse of office politics:
how to survive and thrive in the corporate jungle.

ISBN 1 74114 102 8.

1. Office politics. I. Title.

650.13

Set in 12/13 pt Bembo by Midland Typesetters
Printed by Griffin Press, South Australia

10 9 8 7 6 5 4 3 2 1

FOREWORD

Negative politics in organisations are a waste of people's energy. Office politics take their attention away from their work, distracts them from focusing on the business. By understanding and practising positive politics individuals will find greater job satisfaction—their work will be more fulfilling and interesting. If enough people in an organisation practise positive politics, there will be significant gains in productivity and certainly more harmony.

People are busier meeting ever-increasing pressures than they have ever been, and they must work across many teams and departments to get the necessary results. This means they have to maximise their energies and look for ways to leverage off each other's skills and abilities. The message in *The Use and Abuse of Office Politics* encourages people to develop synergistic relationships to achieve this leverage. This means being 'street smart' in the way you achieve both personal and organisational goals—practising positive politics is both time and resource efficient.

Defending yourself from political attack is all about how you handle political situations—in a positive or a negative way. Take, for instance, a situation where a second-in-charge is promoted above their current boss. I have seen this happen on a number of occasions. Some people, if not many, might take this opportunity to 'rub their superior's nose in it', setting up a negative political situation. However, it is more important to retain the individual's skills and help them understand they still have a crucial role to play. By putting aside egos and personal agendas you can maintain civility and use the situation to create a positive outcome. There are some very valuable lessons to be learned about positive politics from this situation, and this book explores those lessons.

In the many years I have known Mark Holden I have watched him working with a broad spectrum of people as well as organisations both large and small. He has witnessed

v

and negotiated many political situations, both positive and negative, helping to effect large-scale change management. Mark constantly 'walks the tightrope' between people and cultures, positively influencing others to achieve individual and organisational goals.

Organisations today are in a state of continual change. This can generate an environment of conflict and confusion, ideal for breeding negative politics. People need practical advice and direction from an experienced source to help them work effectively and enhance their career opportunities. *The Use and Abuse of Office Politics* provides the sound advice, insight and wisdom that will help people become successful and promotable.

Robert S. Muscat

CONTENTS

PREFACE

Having worked with people and organisations for over 15 years, I continue to be amazed at the complexities of the human side of enterprise. I have made a career of observing human behaviour but still I shake my head and wonder at the way people interact in the organisational context. The psychodramas, power plays, manipulation and knifings provide a constant source of wonder.

When I first started the research for this book, everyone I spoke to had a story of intrigue and betrayal to tell, but although most people were highly aware of politics in the workplace, no one could successfully define it. Or, more correctly, everyone viewed politics within their organisations in one dimension—as a negative and destructive force. However, personal experience had told me that there were positive elements to politics in the workplace and that those who were good at 'playing the politics' positively were most successful.

The idea that there could actually be such a thing as 'positive politics' emerged after a discussion I had with someone very successful in the corporate business world. I got him to explain to me his mode of operation within the organisation: 'What do you do that makes you successful? How do you relate to people? What things do you avoid doing?' Some of the positive things included never putting people down, always trying to help people achieve their personal goals, making your boss's priorities your priorities.

Some things he suggested to avoid included being purely self-serving, manipulating people, backstabbing and claiming other people's work as your own. It all started to make sense, and the differences between positive and negative politics became clear.

The Use and Abuse of Office Politics seeks to define positive and negative politics clearly and to provide insight into how a person can fast-track their career by practising positive politics. The book offers a model for creating a positive political environment and gives practical advice on increasing levels of influence and improving your chances of promotion by focusing on key areas. It also addresses a number of pressing issues concerning politics in modern organisations: what to do about those who practise negative politics; dealing with being 'different'; coping when you make a tactical mistake.

I hope that by the time you finish reading this book you will not only have a clear understanding of what politics in the workplace is all about, but also see how you can use this information strategically to create a more positive political environment for yourself and significantly advance your career. Applying the information provided, you can control politics in your work environment rather than letting it control you.

No doubt you will relate to many of the stories and anecdotes that appear throughout the book. I am sure that there are enough stories and case studies out there to fill libraries. More than anything else, enjoy, and just maybe you will find something you can use.

Mark Holden
February 1998

These relational webs can help organisations to function smoothly, as they often bypass the bureaucracy and red tape that slows down the decision-making and problem-solving processes.

Stuart and Caroline

Stuart and Caroline met four years ago when they attended a supervisors' training program. They had worked in the same company for over a year but had not dealt with each other in the course of their work. During their training they were teamed in an exercise that involved them making a presentation to the larger group. Both were petrified of speaking in public and found the entire exercise harrowing and traumatic. On the basis of this shared experience they formed a friendship and as they progressed in their careers and found themselves facing a presentation, they would call on each other for moral support. Caroline became the financial accountant for the company and Stuart headed up the research division. When it came time for budget reviews Stuart would always seek Caroline's advice and input to ensure his budgets reflected corporate objectives and initiatives—not surprisingly, they always did.

Relationships like Stuart and Caroline's are extremely positive and valuable to organisations. They improve efficiency and productivity, as individuals co-operate in achieving corporate goals.

Political webs are like spiders' webs—they are easy to traverse if you are adequately equipped and skilled for the job, but for those who have not made the time or effort to develop the right skills, they can mean the death of a career. This is illustrated in a story related to me when I was interviewing a sales executive about the political infighting that was taking place in his organisation.

7

Ian and David

Ian and David were sales directors working for the same company but managing different product lines. David had worked for Ian for two years, until he was promoted. Prior to David's promotion their relationship had been stormy but workable. Following his promotion it was nothing less than disastrous. 'They hated each other's guts. Sorry, but that's the best way to describe it!' explained the sales executive.

The fun really started when a new branch manager was appointed over both of them. Each tried desperately to malign the other to their new boss, each with the open aim of getting the other fired. Both Ian and David lost credibility in the eyes of their staff and 'factions' started to form within each workgroup as people aligned with the combatants. Morale and efficiency took a nosedive. The flow of sales leads between the two sales groups stopped for fear of making one or the other look good in front of the branch manager. A number of valuable employees left to join the competition as a result of the infighting. In the end Ian was retrenched, taking with him years of price-less knowledge and experience. Both sales teams were in disarray and the organisation lost significant market share. As the sales executive I was interviewing put it succinctly, 'It's a pity neither of them could find something better to do . . .'.

So the political web can be used 'for evil as well as for good'. The informal networks and relationships that make up political webs are often more powerful than the formal lines of reporting and authority depicted in 'org charts'.

As the political web is by nature informal, so are its methods of communication. Personal chats are rarely docu-mented; they do not appear in the company minutes. Quite often discussions take place anywhere but in an office or boardroom—discreet conversations on the telephone, around the coffee machine, in the powder room or on the golf course. Vince, a coffee shop owner operating across the road from a large multinational, provided some interesting insight on this point, 'Most of the really important stuff gets decided over a cappuccino,' he claims. 'There are always groups of two or three people in here with their heads together talking in whispers. I know something really big is going down when they call ahead to book the corner booth.'

Anyone who opens their eyes will see the political web in operation all around them at any time of the day—or night, for that matter.

Six ways to use the political web to your advantage

1. Become an astute observer of the network of relationships that exists around you.
2. Become friendly with lots of people at different levels within the organisation.
3. Identify those people who may be of assistance to you in the future and actively work on getting to know them.
4. Offer support and information to a wide range of people.
5. When developing relationships, focus on areas of shared interests and goals—don't focus on differences.
6. Avoid unnecessary conflict.

Two faces of politics at work

Attitudes towards politics in the workplace vary greatly but it seems most people consider it one of those necessary evils that must be tolerated. The results of the research in Table 1 support this claim. Of the survey's respondents:

- 100 per cent either strongly agreed or agreed that politics is a common phenomena in most organisations
- 85 per cent either strongly agreed or agreed that you have to be political to get ahead in an organisation
- 67 per cent either strongly agreed or agreed that organisations would be happier places to work without politics.

9

Almost every person surveyed described their political situation in negative terms. On the other hand, very few could articulate any positive actions they were taking to improve their personal political environment. This is not to say that there is no concerted effort by people to improve their political environment; what it does say is that there is minimal 'big picture' awareness of their current political environment compared to their desired future political environment. *Not one* of the hundreds of people I have spoken to on this topic had developed a coherent strategy that would take them towards political success.

Before developing this kind of strategy it is essential to establish that there are two types of politics at work within organisations—negative politics and positive politics. Some people might argue that it is just a matter of semantics, particularly in the case of positive politics—that people are doing positive things all the time to enhance their careers. This is true. However, it is important to see our actions in context. While we hurry to criticise acts of negative politics, we fail to recognise the value of actively practising positive politics. If there is one message that permeates this book, it is *Practise Positive Politics*—and be proactive and strategic in how you go about it.

> ## Practise positive politics—be proactive and strategic.

What is negative politics?

Of the two, negative politics needs the least introduction. We are all aware of how it works and have all at some stage been a victim. Negative politics is

> *the manipulation of the behaviour of others with the sole purpose of achieving personal gain at the expense of individual or organisational goals.*

It is all about self-interest, personal gain and the end justifying the means. Negative politics is a black art, practised in

10

the shadows and stairwells of organisations. Epitomised by whispers and backstabbing, collusion and betrayal, it conjures up images of the worst scenes from *Macbeth* or Dante's *Inferno*. Inevitably good and honest people get hurt by the power plays and manipulations of negative politics, which often destroy self-esteem and confidence and significantly affect career, family and relationships. There is no excuse for the practice of this black art—it is evil and wrong and unnecessary, yet unenlightened human beings still think it is the best way to gain personal advantage.

> # Never be tempted to get involved in the games of negative politics.

Raal

Raal worked as a finance director in a medium-sized banking company. He was responsible for 45–50 people who performed the core functions of the department. Raal himself formed part of the senior management team, along with seven of his peers. On the surface, and particularly in the presence of senior management, Raal seemed very professional, intelligent, considered and personable. His contribution at meetings was balanced and valuable and his interaction with his peers seemed amiable. Outside of these circles, however, Raal was known throughout the organisation as 'The Animal', a reference to his ruthless propensity to play politics and to 'burn' whoever stood in the way of his personal goals. It was common knowledge that Raal wanted to head the organisation and that he would stop at nothing to achieve this goal.

Performance reviews and the production of figures for the annual report were due at roughly the same time and Raal saw an opportunity for him to significantly improve his position in the eyes of the CEO through the manipulation of events. By asking a few discreet questions he was able to identify that the final figures for the annual

11

report were due on the CEO's desk the evening before he was due to have his performance review and scheduled to go to print that same day. He also knew that Kevin, a peer on the senior management team and responsible for the annual report figures, was in conflict with the CEO over some sloppy figures he had passed on only a week before. Having worked in Kevin's area prior to being promoted to his current role, Raal knew his way around the department and its computers very well. The night before the figures were due, he entered Kevin's department and produced his own set of 'wrong' figures and the next evening substituted his figures for Kevin's as they sat on the desk of the CEO's secretary.

When Raal arrived for his performance review the next morning all hell was breaking loose. The CEO's secretary advised Raal that it was unlikely his review would take place as there were problems with the annual report figures. Raal took the opportunity to put his head into the CEO's office.

'Sorry about having to postpone your review, Raal. These annual report figures are all over the place and Kevin isn't in yet.'

'Do you want me to go over them for you, Peter? I used to do those figures when I was in that department, so it wouldn't take me long.'

'It is Kevin's problem and he should really deal with it.'

'OK, just thought I'd offer. When are they due at the printer?'

'God, they're due today. How long do you think it would take you to check through them?'

'If it's the same as usual, about two or three hours.'

'Look, why don't you do that. Keep it to yourself and don't mention it to Kevin, I'll deal with him later. We've really got to get these figures out or the shareholders will be on my tail. Thanks, Raal.'

Raal took the figures down to his office and as he locked the door he told his secretary that he did not want to be disturbed by anyone for the next two hours. He then

12

proceeded to put his feet up on his desk and read the paper. Two hours later he walked out of his office up to the CEO and triumphantly placed Kevin's figures on his desk.

'Done,' he said.

The CEO took his time checking the figures to ensure they were accurate. Eventually he took off his glasses and put the papers down.

'That's more like it. Did you check these figures against the model?'

'I happened to have kept a copy of the software on my computer.'

'Thank goodness for that. You're a lifesaver, Raal, I want you to know that I really appreciate your help with this. I would also appreciate your discretion concerning your involvement while I sort out the situation with Kevin.'

'Peter, that's guaranteed. We're all a team anyway, so it makes little difference as far as I'm concerned.'

'I appreciate your attitude but some things cannot be left unspoken.'

Three weeks later, when the performance reviews had been completed, there had been a management reshuffle. Kevin took on an obscure role in a completely separate division of the company, located on the other side of town. Raal was given the responsibility of taking charge of Kevin's old department as well as his own.

People who actively practise the black art of negative politics are almost obsessively driven by a number of key motivators:

- *ambition*—the need to achieve and be better than everyone else
- *power*—the need to control their own circumstances and environment by controlling others
- *greed*—the need to satisfy the desire for material gain
- *ego*—the need to feel self-important and superior to others

13

- *success*—the need to avoid failure at all costs
- *status*—the need to hold a position of importance and authority.

All of these motivators come with their own psychological baggage that explains such overt political behaviour. The common factor for all who practise this art is the use of win/lose strategies, that is, 'I win/you lose'. For them, there is no other way to play the game. It is wise to be aware of the common methodologies used in the application of these win/lose strategies as you tiptoe your way through the organisational minefield. While the techniques used may vary, the core strategies remain the same.

Four core methodologies of negative politics

1. *Opportunism*—applying the 'kick them while they're down' theory. People who practise negative politics never miss an opportunity to reinforce failure in others with the notion that by doing this they are supporting their own cause.

2. *Brown nosing*—for those involved in negative politics this becomes an art form. They are consummate performers when it comes to professional posturing and corporate voguing for senior management.

3. *Misinformation*—sowing inaccurate or distorted information about people or circumstances is common in negative politics. Practitioners will muddy the waters or sow doubt regarding competence, loyalty or honesty in such a way to make themselves look like heroes.

4. *Power plays*—this method is probably the one from which people who practise negative politics derive the most pleasure. It involves using some kind of force, whether it be position power, the threat of withholding information or the threat of revealing certain information, building a critical mass of opposition or refusing to give their support. It means controlling others in order to control their own environment.

What is positive politics?

Although positive politics consistently works within organisations at a subconscious level, we need to raise it to a more conscious level and develop purposeful strategies to encourage its principles. Positive politics is

the ability to influence the behaviour of others with the purpose of achieving the shared goals of the individuals involved as well as those of the organisation.

Positive politics aligns well with emerging new organisational philosophies and structures. Where negative politics operates best in organisations that are authoritarian, highly structured and hierarchical, positive politics is best suited to organisations that have flatter structures or operate as functional and cross-functional teams, embracing the notions of co-operation, empowerment and ownership. Positive politics focuses on adding value to relationships within organisations—developing allies not saboteurs. It is about identifying mutual goals and developing win/win/win strategies that meet the needs of three key players: the influencer, other individuals and the organisation.

Negative politics supports the adage 'the ends justify the means', but positive politics does not, paying equal attention both to the methods used and the value to be gained by all the parties involved.

Build positive relationships by offering help and support to others as often as possible.

Nina
As part of Nina's responsibilities for human resource development, the general manager gave her the task of upgrading PC skills across the organisation. Initially she outsourced the training to a range of providers, which

turned out to be a very costly exercise. It quickly became obvious that it would be far more cost effective to set up a PC training centre and bring the training inhouse. The challenge she faced was raising the capital expenditure required to buy the equipment needed to finance this venture. In discussions with her GM, he made it clear that while this was a sound idea they had just started a new financial year and the capital expenditure budget did not allow for it. Unless she could find some other way of financing it, the project would have to wait.

Nina decided to arrange lunch with Louise, the information technology manager, with the hope of somehow tapping into the IT capex budget. Over lunch, they discussed how their departments were progressing and some of the individual challenges they were facing. Louise talked at length about the problems she was having in the area of PC support. It seemed that the influx of PCs into the workplace was placing inordinate pressure on her support team. She was going to have to employ two more people to cope with the workload, which was inconvenient as she really needed to put on a couple of new programmers. Nina took this opportunity to raise the issue of inhouse PC training.

'If the staff were better trained in the application software wouldn't that reduce the pressure on your support team?'

'Ultimately, yes. The problem is that my support team can only just keep pace with solving the problems. They don't have time to actually teach people anything. The only solution I can see is to put on more staff.'

'Well, maybe I can help solve your problem.'

Nina then outlined her idea of setting up an inhouse PC training centre to raise staff skill levels. She relayed her discussions with the GM and the problems she was having with capex.

'Louise, I know you have a considerable budget for both hardware and software. What if we worked together? You provide me with the equipment I need to set up this training centre, and I will work to raise the skill level of staff in the priority areas you identify. That way, you won't need to employ any more support staff and can invest that money in programmers. I'll get more value from my training budget and at the same time meet the objectives the GM has set for me.'

Nina and Louise arranged a meeting with the GM to present their idea and outline the savings it would generate for each cost centre. The GM was pleased, as the idea was an effective utilisation of resources for both areas and did not disturb the overall capex budget so early in the financial year. It also enhanced the overall skill levels of staff and procured IT resources for the areas they were most needed.

Both Nina and Louise walked away from the meeting feeling very positive about the value they had added to their departments and the advantages their idea would bring to the organisation.

Positive politics embraces the skills required to success-fully create and traverse the political webs that exist within organisations and helps to structure a positive political environment.

The key motivators of those practising positive politics are:

- *results*—the need to achieve clearly defined goals by working closely with others
- *job satisfaction*—the need to work in a positive and productive environment
- *shared goals*—the need to work as part of a team rather than in isolation, helping others achieve their goals
- *vision*—the need to contribute toward the 'big picture' objectives of the organisation
- *contribution to others*—the need to help others grow and realise their potential
- *relationships*—the need to develop long-lasting profes-sional relationships of mutual benefit.

While these motivators may seem to be idealistic, a closer look will reveal that they reflect emerging and future organisational environments. This gives positive politics relevance, now and in the future, for those wanting to build a successful career.

Four core methodologies of positive politics

1. *Networking*—developing contacts and acquaintances throughout organisations and across industries. It's about developing two-way relationships that are mutually beneficial.

2. *Positive self-marketing*—there are a lot of people out there who are willing to put you down but not a lot who will sing your praises. If you don't, who will? A fine line exists between self-marketing and self-aggrandisement, so there is great value in developing the skill of promoting yourself in a positive, non-aggressive way.

3. *Professionalism*—this is perhaps an overused term, but when building a positive political environment it is important to conduct yourself in a highly professional manner. Do what you do well, always follow through, do what you say you will and don't let people down. People have extremely long and vivid memories.

4. *Sow without a view to reaping*—when it comes to offering information, or giving advice and support, do it freely and with no strings attached. Not everyone for whom you do a favour will necessarily do one in return, but over time you will grow a critical mass of goodwill that will return to you.

> **Do what you do well, always follow through, do what you say you will and don't let people down.**

Politically streetwise

Over the years I have observed a multitude of psycho-political dramas unfolding in hundreds of workplaces. The complex interplays between warring personalities, factions and cliques can become confusing and draining. At the end of the day, these dramas distract us from doing our 'real work', reducing our efficiency and productivity. They just absorb too much emotional and intellectual energy. If you can step back and view your political environment with a little distance the understanding and insight you will gain will enable you to make more informed decisions about your own actions and behaviour. This is 'getting wisdom' about organisational politics.

Edward de Bono, in his book *Textbook on Wisdom*, defines wisdom as the ability to see the big picture and understand how all of the individual parts combine and influence each other to make the whole. Part of understanding the big picture is being able to identify the players in the game, whose characteristics are summarised in Table 2. Consider your political environment as a continuum, where at one end the environment is non-political and at the other end negative politics is rife. Figure 3 shows this political spectrum.

Figure 3 Politically streetwise

NON POLITICAL   + ve   NEGATIVE POLITICS

ANDROIDS   POLITICALLY STREETWISE   HUSTLERS

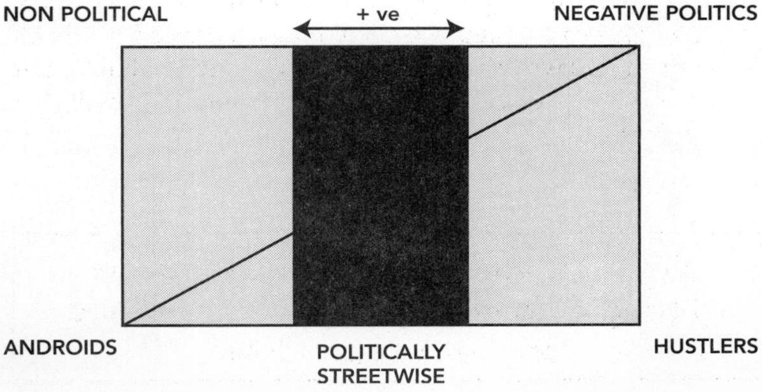

The non-political players are those who have chosen not to be involved in any sort of 'game playing'—the androids. There is nothing wrong with being an android. Many people use work simply as a means to achieve their other goals in life. Annie, for example, worked as an office support person for an exporting firm, but her passion was music. Three or four nights a week she would perform with her bands in pubs and clubs all over the city. She had no desire or ambition to be promoted or to grow in her role as it would interfere with her music. She was competent at what she did at work, but had deliberately chosen a job that was not very demanding. She was an android—come to work, do what you need to do, do it well, go home and get on with life.

There are, of course, androids who have no ambition or desire to achieve anything specific. Unlike Annie, who had a passion beyond her work, these people are happy just to work and live, full stop. There is nothing wrong with making such a choice for your life. The point is that androids are not active participants in the political webs of organisations.

On the other end of the continuum are the hustlers. These are the organisational snakeoil merchants who peddle stories, innuendo, rumour and misinformation, all with the goal of self-promotion. They are always looking for an angle that will

Table 2 The political players

The androids	The streetwise	The hustler
Quiet	Competent	Self-interested
Limited ideas or input	High credibility and respect	Withhold information
Small group of friends	Generally well liked	Manipulative
Unambitious	Wide network of contacts	Controlling
Plodder	Supportive	Coercive
Reliable	Sociable	Egotistical
Often has outside interests	Co-operative	Unenthusiastic towards the success of others

gain them an advantage. Always sucking up, always putting others down, always working the angles—they are virtuosos of the black art of negative politics. It is the hustlers that make life miserable, causing stress and tension for all and sundry.

Between the androids and the hustlers are the politically streetwise, the people who are ambitious and have the drive to get ahead, and who have the skills to create for themselves a positive political environment. They refuse to use the tactics that hustlers employ, but achieve their goals by aligning with the goals of others. These people know who the players are, they know the nature of their political environment—they are, in other words, streetwise.

Understanding this political continuum will help you identify where you lie between the androids and hustlers. Once you have done this, you can start developing a strategy to improve your political environment by practising positive politics.

Pulling it all together

We have established that dealing with organisational politics is an integral part of career success. We have viewed the two faces of politics—positive and negative. The question that now begs to be answered is:

How can you create for yourself a positive political environment that will work to your advantage?

The simple model on the following page contains the essential components required to develop your strategy for shaping a positive political environment. We can call it the 2P model—for Positive Politics.

Let's look at each of the 2P model's components.

Competence, confidence, credibility and trust

The two core components of any career are competence and confidence. Firstly, you must be competent at what you do in order to be taken seriously. You must be able to do the

21

Figure 4 The 2P model

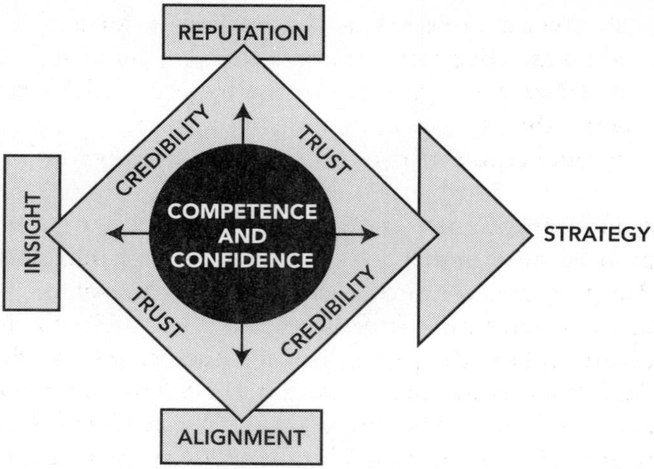

basics of your job and do them well. If there is any question asked by either your management or peers regarding your effectiveness you will not be taken seriously. Incompetence will undermine your credibility on every front and bring into doubt any ideas and suggestions you may present regardless of how good or effective they are. The rules here are, always:

- do your job as well as, or preferably better than anyone else
- deliver on time
- be thorough and cover all of the bases
- make your manager's priorities your priorities
- present problems with solutions in mind.

Coupled with competence is confidence. Confidence is strongly aligned with a positive professional self-image. Confidence relies on belief in your professional capabilities and in your ability to deliver the goods just as well as, if not better than your peers. There is a very fine line between confidence and arrogance, and in future chapters this is explored in more detail to ensure you avoid such pitfalls.

22

The basic rules when building confidence are:

- never express self-doubt in a public forum
- be assertive when expressing ideas and opinions
- always back your arguments with sound reasoning
- be direct
- only argue strongly if you know you will win.

How many times have you seen one of your peers gain a promotion or added responsibilities and thought, 'I'm better than they are at my work. Why was the promotion offered to them and not me'? In many cases it is matter of perception. Based on how the person presents themselves and the confidence they exude, the manager may perceive them to be more effective in their role. Projecting a confident and professional image is important when building positive perceptions about your capabilities and the value you offer the organisation.

Being seen to be competent and confident in the performance of your work responsibilities and your relationships with others builds credibility and trust. Credibility and trust are highly valuable tokens of trade when dealing in the political environments of organisations. This is true from both a professional and personal viewpoint. If you are perceived as being believable and honest (credible), and reliable and responsible (trustworthy), managers will rely upon you more than upon others. Peers and members of your team will seek your advice and input and often take you into their confidence.

Being competent and confident builds trust and credibility—these are the core components required to develop for yourself a positive political environment.

Reputation

Once you have a sound base of competence, confidence, credibility and trust, you can move on to the more strategic activities of consciously building your reputation. Building a good reputation means amassing positive credit to your name. People who consistently practise negative politics

23

typically build for themselves a bad reputation. On the other hand, if you consistently apply the principles of positive politics, you will build yourself a good reputation.

A good reputation involves:

- being held in high esteem
- exhibiting behaviours that generate approval
- gaining respect from your colleagues
- displaying a sound and reliable character
- doing things for individuals and the organisation that are commendable.

Your reputation is in some ways dependent on the culture and values of the organisation in which you are working. A good reputation in one organisation may well be perceived as a bad reputation in another. It is therefore important to understand the culture, values and priorities that exist within an organisation's culture.

In following chapters we will discuss in detail exactly how you can strategically build yourself a good reputation and align with the culture of your organisation.

Alignment

How effective is your 'political web'? Another key component to consider when creating for yourself a positive political environment is the effectiveness of the personal affiliations you develop within your organisation. Alignment is about building a network of contacts and relationships with people in your organisation who can help you achieve your goals.

Useful and effective alignments are built by:

- doing favours and extracting favours
- win/win/win strategies
- helping and supporting others
- establishing common goals and objectives
- finding common social ground
- sharing power, information and resources
- friendship, loyalty and partnership.

The old adage 'it's not what you know but who you know' comes to mind when talking about alignments and in many ways this is true. However, in light of our previous discussions regarding competence and confidence, this adage would better serve our purposes if it read, 'it is what you know, but who you know can make life a damn sight easier'.

Developing a wide network of people who are positively disposed to help you wherever they can provides a smooth, or at least smoother, path towards your goals. People who thrive on adversarial relationships are only building mountains for themselves in the long run. One senior manager offered his philosophy: 'If I come head to head with someone in a confrontation I have one simple response—I take a huge step forward.' And he lived by this philosophy. There came a time in his career when he needed considerable public support in order for a project to be accepted. Not surprisingly, when he turned around to see who was willing to put their neck on the line—guess what?—no one was there.

It is essential to build a 'web' of positive personal relationships strategically and with sincerity to have a successful career.

Insight

An old proverb admonishes, 'In all your getting, get wisdom.' Earlier in this chapter we saw that de Bono defines wisdom as the ability to see the big picture and understand how all of the individual parts combine and influence each other to make the whole. The component of the model we call insight is all about gaining wisdom in two areas:

- the organisation
- its people.

The organisation

To be successful in the practice of positive politics you need to have a big picture understanding of your organisation and its various functions. You will need to know:

25

- the organisation's overall business objectives, how your department helps to meet those objectives and ultimately how you will contribute to these objectives
- the nature of the organisation's culture
- the organisation's core values
- the behaviours that are rewarded and those which are frowned upon
- where the power bases lie.

This big picture insight will help you to fine tune your activities until they are in line with the things that really matter to the organisation. Your work will consequently have more relevance and you will gain a higher profile.

People

The organisation is the people. As basic as this statement may seem, it contains a fundamental premise that is often overlooked or given insufficient attention. To be able to create for yourself a positive political environment you must have two things:

- a clear understanding of your personal behavioural make up—what makes you tick
- an understanding of the behavioural make up of others—what makes them tick.

You do not need to become a pseudo-psychologist, but there is real personal and professional value and advantage to be gained from having a deep insight into why people behave the way they do. This insight into people will help you:

- develop stronger relationship webs
- know what 'hot buttons' to press to influence which people
- gain support from a wide range of individuals, not just the ones you naturally get along with
- deal more strategically and effectively with management on a personal basis.

Such insight will help you project a more mature and measured approach to your work and the way you deal with people. It will assist you in the development of a sound strategy for creating that positive political environment.

Strategy

The 'strategy' part of the model involves analysing your current position, projecting your future position and determining how you are going to get there.

As you go through this book, you'll find out how to analyse your current:

- competence
- confidence
- credibility and trust
- reputation
- alignment
- insight.

Then you can project what you would like your situation to look like in each of these areas. From there we will develop sound strategies for you to implement that will help you improve your current political environment.

Remember:

- It *is* possible for you to positively influence those around you
- It *is* possible for you to control how people view your contribution
- It *is* possible for you to enhance your chances of career success through creating a positive political environment.

Here is a quick activity to help you think about your current political environment.

27

How political is your work environment?

This is a questionnaire to help you identify the level and kinds of politics existing in your workplace. As you complete these questions, think of your organisation or department under *normal* circumstances and try to answer as realistically as possible.

Below are two opposing descriptions relating to the work environment with a rating scale in between. Think about each description and circle the number that best identifies where your organisation lies between the two.

Co-operative and supportive	1 2 3 4 5 6 7 8 9 10	Unco-operative and self-interested
Positive social environment	1 2 3 4 5 6 7 8 9 10	Little social interaction
Team oriented	1 2 3 4 5 6 7 8 9 10	Focused on individual tasks
Harmonious	1 2 3 4 5 6 7 8 9 10	Confrontational
Trust	1 2 3 4 5 6 7 8 9 10	Suspicion
Group decision making	1 2 3 4 5 6 7 8 9 10	Individual power bases
Team goals	1 2 3 4 5 6 7 8 9 10	Personal agendas
Celebration of individual successes	1 2 3 4 5 6 7 8 9 10	Individual successes ignored
Cohesive workgroup	1 2 3 4 5 6 7 8 9 10	Cliques
Shared information	1 2 3 4 5 6 7 8 9 10	Withheld information
Total:		

Add up the numbers you have circled and refer to the score interpretation.

Score	Interpretation
10–25	Positive political environment with normal levels of interaction
26–50	Some negative politics existing but among only a few individuals
51–75	Strong undercurrents of negative politics making your work environment uncomfortable
76–100	High levels of overt negative politics affecting your work environment

Chapter 2

A MODEL FOR UNDERSTANDING POLITICS AT WORK

BUILD A POSITIVE POLITICAL ENVIRONMENT

> If you have built castles in the air, your work
> need not be lost; that is where they should be.
> Now put foundations under them.
>
> Henry David Thoreau

A few years back I bought a house that needed a fair bit of renovation. Actually, it needed a hell of a lot of renovation. Moreover, the backyard was a jungle. When I started to clear some of this jungle, I discovered a reasonably sized garden shed. The best place for this shed was in the very back corner of the yard, but before I could move it, I had to build some sort of a foundation to put it on. My first thought was to forget building a foundation at all. Just move it and put it on the bare ground. Then logic took control and despite the fact I had hundreds of other pressing things I needed to do, I decided to approach the business properly. So, I levelled the ground, dug the foundations, put in a solid concrete slab— then moved the shed. Looking back on the exercise, I'm glad that I made the effort and did it properly at the start, otherwise it would have cost me a lot of extra time, effort and money.

The importance of foundations is an accepted notion of our everyday thinking. If you want something to last you start by building strong foundations. The bigger the structure you want to build, the stronger and deeper the foundations need to be. The problem most of us have with foundations is that a lot of time is spent working on something for which we see little short-term progress. Have you seen a construction company start to build a highrise only to have a 'hole in the ground' for what seems to be years? Then, 'all of a sudden' the building takes shape and seems to be finished 'overnight'.

Foundation building is one of life's principles—if you want some thing to last and retain the possibility of growth and expansion—*build solid foundations*! Foundations also play an extremely important role when building yourself a positive political environment. In Chapter 1 we saw that there are four foundational components you need to develop thoroughly before you consider doing anything else:

- competence
- confidence
- credibility
- trust.

Ignoring these foundational components within the political context will limit your career growth and promotional potential. They are the essential starting points for your ability to exert influence within your organisation. Chapter 2 looks at these components in some detail and provides you with practical ways of developing each.

Figure 5 Trust and credibility

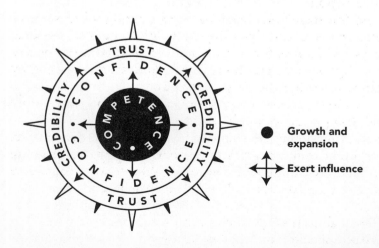

Competence

To effectively create a positive political environment you must first and foremost be competent in your particular area of skill or expertise. Competence is being:

- properly qualified
- able to do a task
- efficient
- suitable.

Whether you are in office support, sales, architecture, marketing, medicine or law, unless you gain a reputation for being competent in your field you will find it extremely difficult to establish the credibility and trust required to be noticed. However, once you are known for being competent, people will begin to trust your judgement and the ideas, suggestions and comments you make will take hold in an atmosphere of credibility and trust. Getting ideas accepted is the beginning of your ability to exert influence. To the degree that you are perceived to be competent and to the degree that you build credibility and trust, to the same degree you will be able to exert influence. And it is influence that oils the wheels of the machine of positive politics in organisations.

At this stage you are probably wondering what role *confidence* plays in this all star line-up. Confidence is the personal 'sales' mechanism for you and your abilities. There is no use being good at something unless you have the means by which to communicate your 'greatness'.

At the beginning of your career competence is the only tool you possess to start building a positive political environment. Your ability to do the basics well and deliver reliable, consistent results on time is the best thing you have going for you. As you become more established, you accumulate other strings to your 'influence' bow, such as:

- qualifications you have achieved
- companies you have worked for

31

- positions you have held
- projects you have accomplished
- contacts you have made.

But in the early days your focus must be on being competent at what you have been employed to do. Once you have mastered the basics, the next thing to focus on is 'standing out from the crowd', that is, being better than your peers at what you do.

Standing out from the crowd

Looking better than your peers is easy if you work with a gaggle of turkeys, but what if the people you work with are just as competent as you or, for that matter, more competent? It becomes a matter of consistently doing the right things and 'producing the goods' in a way that aligns with your manager's priorities and goals. Let's have a look at a range of practical things you can do to project a competent image in the workplace and stand out from the crowd.

Get it right

There is no substitute for a sound grasp of the basics regardless of the industry or profession in which you work. When you finish school or complete your degree and start doing 'real work' you might think, 'Gee, I wish I had paid more attention in that accounting (or English, or maths, or . . .) class'. And maybe you should have. The basics should come as second nature. You should be able to do them without thinking. In the corporate world fools are not suffered lightly and stupidity certainly doesn't help to build credibility and trust. If you consistently make mistakes that relate to the basics you are sure to be tagged a loser and allotted mundane and 'foolproof' tasks. So get the fundamentals right!

Sound technical knowledge

If you're a mathematician, know your algebra; if you're an accounts payable clerk, know your companies systems; if you're a printer, know how to mix ink; if you're a doctor, don't leave a sponge in the patient. Whatever it is you do, there are a range of standard principles, models, processes, systems and techniques that your profession uses to ensure a basic level of competence. There is no excuse for not knowing these fundamentals and standards.

Usually you cannot operate in a particular field unless you have studied it—that doesn't mean that some people still don't get it wrong. We have all been exposed to someone who doesn't know the basic techniques of their job. It does not inspire you with confidence and respect, does it? If you are a bit rusty on the basic techniques drag out the old text books and brush up. Even better, buy some of the newer text books and find out the latest trends and techniques. If you have been thrown into a role for which you are not trained (and you would be surprised how often this happens—how many people are *trained* in management, for example, before they are given a management role?), don't continue to stumble around blindly 'learning from your mistakes'. Go back to college, do a training course, read some books on the subject, find yourself a mentor, join a professional association—whatever you do make sure you are competent in the basic technical requirements of your job.

> ## Don't stumble around blindly 'learning from your mistakes'. Go back to college, do a training course, read some books . . .

Accuracy

There is nothing worse than handing over a piece of work only to have your manager point out a spelling error in the first paragraph or, cringe, in the heading. Other phrases that send a chill down the spine:

- 'These figures don't seem to add up.'
- 'Weren't you supposed to include . . .'

33

- 'We don't *have* a branch office in . . .'
- 'What about the x phase of the project?'

Being accurate most, if not all, of the time enhances the perception that you are competent at what you do. Imagine you had to make a choice between two people to do a very important and urgent piece of work for you. Bill—who does know what he is doing but is careless and consistently needs to have his work corrected, and Hari—who is as good at her job and rarely makes a mistake. It is a 'no brainer'.

Check and doublecheck your work. Get someone else to go over it for you if necessary, but *never* hand in work that is likely to be subject to error.

Conciseness

Another aspect of competence is the ability to be concise. Most managers are finely tuned to the 'fudge factor'. Ever been in a meeting where the manager asks a colleague a question only to be met by a meandering, circuitous 'answer'? By the time they have finished talking nobody is quite sure what the question was. This is called 'fudging' and is designed to cover up areas of incompetence or a lack of knowledge. Politicians are experts at this technique. If you are competent you can afford to be concise by giving succinct answers and information that is devoid of waffle. Where there is a need for more detailed information, your manager will ask for it and you, of course, will be able to give it. Managers appreciate information communicated in this way—it saves a lot of time. By highlighting only the salient points you present the scope of the information; and where your manager asks questions, you can provide the depth that is required. This is a quality exercised by highly competent operators that builds respect and credibility: 'That Clayton really knows his stuff!'.

Cohesion

Cohesion is all about making sense, making sure that everything you do is connected and 'hangs together'. One very

34

talented presenter and facilitator is an example of the importance of cohesion. Unfortunately, presenting and facilitating were only about 20 per cent of his job. The rest of the time he was responsible for planning, coordinating, consulting and following through on client requests. If he was very good at the 20 per cent, he was hopeless at the 80 per cent. Not that he couldn't perform each individual task—he just lacked the ability to pull it all together and consistently connect all of the parts. He'd promise things and forget to follow through; he'd fail to communicate important information; he'd do it well one time and badly the next. After only a few months, he lost so much credibility with his customers that they were referring to him as 'Mr Incredible'. Bad sign. He was encouraged to find another job.

Cohesion is about being aware of all your job's component tasks and making sure they all connect in a logical way. It is about following through, and covering all the possibilities. Its about being knowledgeable about all of the resources at your disposal and using them to your advantage. It's about presenting your ideas and solutions in a way that hangs together.

Consistency

'Consistency thou art a jewel.' So Shakespeare said, and how right he was. John is rarely up to anything too demanding every second Friday, because he gets paid on the Thursday and goes drinking with his mates all night. Alison is so emotionally unstable after a long string of volatile relationships that she is in tears most of the time. Work? Oh yeah, sorry, forgot about that!

Performance can be affected by so many different internal and external factors that when a manager finds someone who actually produces a high standard of work on a consistent basis they are indeed a jewel. Being consistently accurate, consistently on time, consistently logical, consistently thorough—these go a long way to establishing your credibility and trust. In fact you could well make yourself invaluable. Now that would certainly help your ability to influence.

It is this kind of behaviour that will help you 'stand out from the crowd' and establish yourself as a competent and valuable employee.

Emma

Emma was 22 when she started her new job as a credit clerk in the accounting department of a manufacturing company. She knew that she was on the bottom rung of the ladder but was determined to make something of her career and to progress as far as she possibly could within her organisation. It took her a while to learn the basics of her job and although it wasn't ideal, she continued to consider what she was doing as a stepping stone to the future. She noticed that the general attitude of her workmates was 'do as little as you can get away with and then slow down a bit', and decided that if she took the opposite stance it could only make her look good.

Emma ensured that any work she was given was done quickly and accurately, and when she had nothing to do she would help someone else with their work or ask her team leader for more work to do. A number of her workmates seemed to resent her efforts and quietly advised her to slow down a bit—'it's making us look bad'. But Emma didn't heed their advice.

She would often volunteer to do the work that everyone else found boring or arduous, she would only take short lunch breaks and she made it a point never to make the same mistake twice. Her contribution at team meetings was consistently valuable and she was always looking for ways to improve the way things were done.

Her efforts did not go unnoticed and although she had been with the company less than a year, the department manager decided to promote her into a team leader's position. This move stirred up a bit of unrest among Emma's workmates, giving her some moments of angst when she took over the responsibility of being their team leader. For a while some of her team gave her a particularly hard time about being their 'boss' and her limited time with the organisation. Despite her inexperience, Emma handled them well and soon had them all on side and working positively toward common goals.

Now part of the management team in her department, Emma had the opportunity to lobby for changes she had always felt would improve productivity and efficiency. There were a few other things she had in mind to suggest to change as well—given time she was confident she could influence the management team. She did.

Emma studied accounting and a few years and a few organisations later, had successfully worked her way into a senior accounting role that paid a good salary. Many of the people she had worked with in the credit department in her first job were still there—no surprise really.

> **Build political credit by accepting unpleasant tasks, doing favours for others and volunteering to work the extra hours.**

This story illustrates some ways to establish your competence. It also suggests some of the political problems you can face when you decide to take positive steps to build your career. Navigating your way through such situations can be stressful and cause you some anxiety. However, here are some practical things you can do if you are faced with this sort of political situation:

- let your team know that you are new to these responsibilities and will need their help
- recognise the unique talents, knowledge and experience of those in the team and encourage them to contribute
- work with the team and individuals to set goals that measure feedback and performance on a regular basis
- get some input from your manager on the different personalities in your team

37

- keep the end goal in mind and don't give in to mediocrity
- stay aware of what is happening and *privately* confront those who are giving you trouble
- be firm about what needs to be done but don't ever be aggressive towards individuals.

Focus on the things that matter

If you want to be noticed it is important to identify early your priorities in three key areas:

1. The aspects of your particular job that are perceived to contribute significantly towards your department achieving its goals.
2. The things that are perceived to be valuable in the culture of your department.
3. The things that are important to your manager.

This boils down to how well you use your time and how efficiently you expend your effort.

Your job
A good starting point when determining the things that really matter in your particular job is to go through your position description and look at the key result areas—those major functions you fulfil that specify the results required. If you don't have key result areas for your job, a better starting point would be to talk with your manager and determine what they are. In consultation with your manager, put these in priority order and then determine the percentage of your time you should be allocating to each area. Table 3 shows an example of prioritising job tasks.

This will help you identify what is important to your manager and where you should be spending your time.

Your department
Each department places certain values on different activities. These values usually centre around timeliness, quality and

Table 3 Prioritising your job tasks

Priority	Key result area	Time allocated
1	Responding to customer enquiries	30%
2	Processing order sheets	20%
3	Following up customer complaints	15%
4	Updating customer database	15%
5	Preparing quotes	10%
6	Updating reps' sales information	10%

quantity. Is it more important that you get through large quantities of work or that attention is paid to detail and quality? Is there an emphasis on the presentation of documents or is this of little value? Is there an emphasis on the quality of the relationships you develop with other departments or is there a more external focus on suppliers? Identifying where the values of your department lie will help you determine the things on which you should be concentrating. This will help you 'fit in' and increase the perceived value of your work.

Your manager

There is no doubt that your manager will have goals and preferences that are important to them personally. By identifying these goals and preferences you will be able to target your efforts for maximum effectiveness. There are two maxims you should live by:

1. *Make your manager look good*—if you have to represent your department or prepare materials or documents on behalf of your manager, make sure you do it in a way that will reflect well on them.
2. *Make your manager's priorities your priorities*—if your manager asks you to do something, put it on the top of your priority list. Respond quickly and efficiently and make sure it is done well.

Focusing on the things that really matter in these areas will lift your profile and give greater impact to the things you do.

39

Seek advice

An old proverb states that 'there is wisdom in many counsellors'. When you are given responsibility for an important task or project, talk to a wide range of people seeking input and advice. This will expose you to a range of different views and perspectives that you may not have considered and will give your work greater scope and depth. Choose the people you speak to carefully, based on their reputation and abilities, and make sure you take their advice in the total context of the task you have to perform. Those you talk to don't necessarily have to come from your organisation—a cross-section of people both within and external to your organisation can provide a greater diversity of views. People generally respond positively when asked for their advice, as it appeals to their self-esteem.

A grab bag of ideas

Here are a few more ideas to help you build your levels of competence.

Work hard
Show dedication and focus. Start early and leave work late. Volunteer for extra tasks. Don't take long lunches. Avoid taking 'sickies'.

Do the hard jobs
Don't procrastinate doing those jobs you don't like. Don't complain or whinge about tasks you find unsavoury. If you are really keen, offer to do the hard jobs that other people avoid.

Learn from your mistakes
No one will criticise you for making a mistake but if you continue to make the same mistake you will look like a fool.

Be direct and speak the truth
If you know what you are talking about, you can afford to be strong in stating your convictions. Stand up for your

principles but give in on those things that don't really matter. Never get involved in arguments that you can't win.

Work within the system

Those who continually fight the system are seen as 'hard to manage'. This is frustrating and perplexing to managers, who have a myriad of other things to think about. Get on with 'it' (whatever 'it' may be), make 'it' happen and you will be considered a valuable contributor to the team.

Get results

Managers are consistently trying to strike a balance between getting results and managing people. If you are easy to manage *and* you get the results they are looking for, you will place yourself in a highly advantageous position. This will help you create the 'proven track record' you need and will be taken into account when it comes time for promotion or the allocation of important work.

Quietly perform exceptional tasks

Don't continually go to your manager seeking reassurance. It's OK to get clarification and to occasionally confirm that you are heading in the right direction, but it becomes blindingly obvious when you think you are out of your depth— 'not waving, drowning'. It is better to get input from someone more experienced, do the task well and 'surprise' your manager with exceptional work.

Play it straight

Don't get involved in any of the dirty politics swirling around the office. Get a reputation for being honest and direct. Be a straight shooter and get in the habit of 'telling it like it is'. A no-nonsense approach will automatically be attributed to your work as well. Don't take this to the extreme and become hard, cold and aggressive—just be sure everyone knows where you stand.

Solve routine problems efficiently

Don't doubt your own abilities. If there is a problem that needs to be solved and you have done it, or something

41

similar, before—just do it. Be careful not to overstep your bounds of authority but be confident enough to operate right on the line. Managers see this as having drive and taking initiative, which are the admirable and desirable qualities of the truly competent.

Approach problems with solutions in mind
All day every day managers spend their time dealing with problems. When you walk through their office door and say, 'I've got a problem,' it is the last thing they ever want to hear. If you have to talk to your manager about a problem, make sure that before you do you have a number of alternative solutions up your sleeve. This way you are not dumping them with yet another problem to solve.

Be a finisher
Don't leave things undone. If you are given a task see it through to the end. Don't procrastinate till your manager has to ask for it. Be ahead of the game if possible. Don't meet deadlines, beat deadlines. Some personality types have big problems finishing things. If this is you, get over it. Discipline yourself and make sure you get things done. There is nothing that will make you look more incompetent than holding onto a number of unfinished tasks.

> ## Some personality types have big problems finishing things. If this is you, get over it.

Demonstrate maturity and independence
When you express maturity you demonstrate that you have fully developed your ability to complete a task or role. You have 'grown up', if you like, and can be relied upon and trusted to do your job. Independence is the ability to act alone without supervision or the help of others. Coupled together, maturity and independence are a powerful tool.

Managers love people who are mature and independent—it means they don't have to worry about them. Ensure your behaviour confirms your maturity and independence to management.

Some people may be tempted to think, 'Competence is really all you need in order to make a name for yourself and get ahead in any organisation'. It is true that there is a small number of individuals who are exceptionally talented in their particular area of expertise. They establish such a reputation for themselves, built on their exceptional skills, that they achieve a high profile and their services are in constant demand. I would suggest however that these people represent the exception, not the rule. These people are the boffins, the propeller heads, the geniuses among us—and unfortunately the majority of us cannot claim to fall into such a category. We have to rely on our more basic skills and any other techniques we can muster to help us along the way. Let's now consider how *confidence* coupled with *competence* can accelerate your ability to develop credibility and trust and assist in the creation of your positive political environment.

> **Always maintain the political high ground—and never enter into an argument you can't win.**

Confidence

Black and white television was a new technology when I was a child. I can remember sitting in the lounge room in the dark with my family, the blue-grey flickering light of the TV reflecting on our faces. One of the down sides of this new technology was that occasionally things would go awry. The most common fault was the 'rolling' picture. Dad would thrust one arm behind the unit laying his face flat against its side and twist some mysterious knob at the back while asking 'How's that?'. (I could never work out why the roll knob

43

couldn't be on the front of the TV where you could actually see the screen while you were adjusting it.) I distinctly remember one night when we were all watching the news. The prime minister of the day was part way through an important speech when the sound suddenly went. He continued to read this very important speech but we, of course, could not hear a word he was saying.

If we use this as an analogy to describe the relationship between competence and confidence, competence is the 'important words'—the script of what has to be said— and confidence is the mechanism by which the words are communicated. The sound, if you like. Without his script the prime minister would have looked rather foolish, sitting there with nothing to say. Without the sound, he was mouthing the words but we couldn't hear the important things being said. Competence without confidence has a very similar effect. When the right levels of competence are combined with the right levels of confidence, you have the ingredients to effectively communicate your value and the opportunity to significantly enhance your career.

Confidence in the workplace is:

- self-assurance and belief in your capabilities
- the boldness to assert your knowledge, skills and experience.

Table 4 outlines the key characteristics of confident people.

Laura and Michelle

Laura and Michelle worked in the logistics department of a chemical manufacturing company. Laura had started work one month after Michelle, and both had been there almost three years. Each was as skilled and competent at their work as the other, yet there were some fundamental differences when it came down to their attitude and approach.

Michelle was a quiet and deferential type of person. She didn't like making waves, didn't like to be the centre of attention or controversy, avoided conflict and on most

Table 4 Characteristics of confidence

People who have confidence	People who lack confidence
■ are motivated and at ease with themselves	■ defer to others' opinions
■ are not nervous about their abilities	■ put themselves and their work down
■ put forward their point of view	■ don't take compliments well
■ believe in themselves	■ don't put forward ideas or opinions
■ are not threatened or insecure	■ downplay any contribution
■ recognise their own value and worth	■ can put others down to compensate for their own inadequacies
■ are accepting of others	■ communicate poorly
■ value the contribution of others	■ lack self-motivation
■ recognise and commend the input of others	■ may be reluctant to take on new responsibilities
■ accept compliments graciously	

occasions only gave her opinion when asked. 'I'm paid to come here every day and make sure stock levels are maintained in line with production schedules. That doesn't mean I'm not interested in other things but that must remain my focus and priority.' At meetings she rarely said much or proffered ideas or suggestions. When asked technical questions that related to her job she was always up to speed and capable of answering. Michelle generally lacked confidence.

Laura, on the other hand was very capable and confident, projecting a positive and convincing demeanour. She was sure of herself, assertive in her opinions, direct and often challenged the ideas of others (even her manager at times) with reasonable and logical arguments. She was very hard to intimidate, was always putting forward new ideas and solutions to problems (that usually worked) and was persistent without being too pushy.

Michelle and Laura's manager, Martin, spoke with his manager, Ruth, concerning a promotional opportunity for which they were both being considered.

'So, Martin, who would you contemplate as your most promising candidates for this new team leader role?'

'There is no doubt, Ruth, that Michelle and Laura are the two front-runners. But it will be difficult to choose between them—they are both extremely competent.'

'I agree. They are both very impressive candidates. Let me ask you a few questions to help clarify things. If you needed someone to take control during a crisis who would you choose?'

'I would most likely choose Laura, because she is decisive and can make decisions quickly if she needs to.'

'Of the two, who is willing to stand up to you if they think you are wrong? You don't want a 'yes' person in this role.'

'Well, if you put it that way, it would have to be Laura again. She certainly isn't backward in coming forward and she has challenged my ideas on a number of occasions in the past.'

'Martin, one more question. Of the two, who will provide better leadership for the team?'

'This is starting to sound very one-sided, but it would have to be Laura. She embraces the ideas and opinions of others but is decisive when she needs to be. It seems to be a clear choice really.'

'Yes, I think it does, Martin. I think it does.'

In the end, Laura's confidence gave her a real edge. It gave colour and depth to her skills and made her stand out from her peers. While Michelle was extremely good at her job, her lack of confidence robbed her of the ability to promote herself and establish her potential value in a more senior role.

Where's the balance?

Teaming confidence with competence provides you with leverage when looking at career progress and building credibility and trust. There is, however, a need for a balance between the two. At one end of the continuum someone with lots of competence and little confidence will miss opportunities largely because they go about their work unnoticed. On the other hand, someone who has lots of confidence and little competence will often sell themselves into situations where they cannot cope with the demands, seriously damaging their career progress. Consider the graphs below:

Figure 6 High competence, low confidence

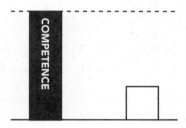

In Figure 6 competence is high and confidence is low. This is the profile of Michelle in the story above. This person is quite capable of doing the job but lacks the confidence to project their capabilities and develop positive perceptions.

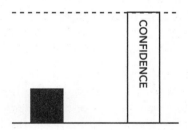

Figure 7 Low competence, high confidence

Figure 7 is the profile of a person who thinks they are good but in fact lacks the competence to do the job effectively. These people may be arrogant and aggressive, and very hard to deal with at any level. This can also be a very dangerous profile, in that the ability of these people to gain the 'confidence' of management is very high and they can often

47

acquire influence they do not deserve. These people are often described as being 'out of their depth' or 'not up to the job'—meaning they are basically incompetent.

Figure 8 High competence, high confidence

Figure 8 is a profile to strive for, where your level of confidence equals your level of competence. You are fully aware of your capabilities, you know what you can and cannot do. This profile would match Laura's in the story above. By practising the techniques covered previously in this chapter you will ensure a positive competence profile. The remainder of this chapter covers techniques to help you develop your confidence profile.

Figure 9 High competence, higher confidence

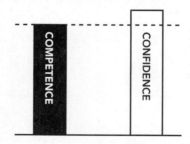

There is one more profile I would like to discuss. Perhaps even more effective than the previous profile is one where your confidence levels are slightly higher than your levels of competence (Figure 9). People who are ambitious and are driving their own career often adapt this profile. Finding themselves being given tasks or promotions slightly out of their reach, they are encouraged to learn, grow and develop by 'stretching' their capabilities. The danger is that they may 'over sell' themselves, ending up in a situation where they lack the basic competencies the job requires. There are no set rules to govern this scenario, so just don't overdo it. Although this could be seen as a high risk strategy for your career, it is still an extremely viable approach. In my own career, I have occasionally 'sold' myself into a role only to ask myself once I got there 'What the hell do I do now?'. This scenario *can* provide you with the opportunity and challenge to grow, but if you are not careful it can also be the launch pad to a major career disaster.

Building confidence

Your confidence levels are closely related to your self-perception or self-esteem and these both have a considerable impact on how you behave. A strong belief in yourself and your abilities will be projected in your behaviour and the people you work with will develop positive perceptions of your capabilities. On the other hand, if you are retiring about your abilities, if you defer or withdraw when challenging tasks are presented, people will start to doubt your capabilities. So your internal view of yourself will ultimately be projected through your behaviour, which will mould the views of others. While it is extremely important to be realistic about your skills and abilities, it is also true that no prizes are given to those who are reluctant to wave their own flag.

Stephen

Stephen had gained a reputation for being extremely competent in his particular field. He worked at middle management level as an account manager for a large advertising agency. He was a quiet man who preferred 'getting on with it' and producing the results rather than 'doing lunch' and 'schmoozing' with the boss. In his own

49

time (and to no one else's knowledge) he had earned his masters degree in Marketing and had been unobtrusively and successfully applying his knowledge. He had started with the agency in an interstate branch and had progressed rapidly early in his career, being promoted every 12 or 18 months and moving a number of times among the agency's other state branches.

Eventually, he secured a position at head office in his current role—this had been three and a half years ago. It seemed he had enjoyed greater influence and projected a better profile in his interstate roles than he could at head office. This had been concerning him for quite a while and his confident expectation of continuing success in head office had faded a little more every time he was overlooked for promotion. I received a call from Stephen requesting a time when we could sit down and discuss his situation and identify some of the road blocks that were limiting his progress. He was noticeably and understandably upset when we started our conversation.

'I'm totally disillusioned at the moment,' he told me. 'I've been at head office for over three years now and I'm going nowhere. I would have been better off staying in the interstate branches—at least I could have been managing one of the offices by now.'

'Stephen, why do you think you were overlooked for that last promotion?'

'Now, I have to say, that is a mystery to me. I'm not putting Marcia down, but I am just as good, if not better than she is, at the job. I have more experience plus I have better qualifications. The only thing I can put it down to is her ability to "suck up" to management, she is always pushing herself into the more interesting and high profile accounts.'

'Don't you think you should consider a similar tactic in order to give yourself a higher profile with management?'

'I could I guess, but it has never been my style. I have always worked on the philosophy that, if you work hard and get the results you won't need to "wave your own flag". You will be recognised for your intrinsic talent. I feel uncomfortable singing my own praises and even more uncomfortable having lunch or playing golf with the bosses when I know my sole intent is self-promotion.'

I spent some time talking to Stephen's managers and gathering their perceptions of him and the value of his work. Their responses to my questions regarding why he was overlooked for promotion went something like this:

- 'Sometimes we forget he's even there.'
- 'We asked ourselves whether he would be assertive enough to manage the role when it really came to the crunch.'
- 'He doesn't seem as confident as others.'
- 'Others seem to have a lot more runs on the board. I'm not sure if that is necessarily true, but it certainly seems that way.'
- 'He's too quiet and retiring.'
- 'He seemed to be far more effective when he was working the interstate branches.'

When I analysed these responses they all fell into the category of perceptions. Stephen was not *perceived* to be as confident, successful or capable as his peers—therefore, as far as his management was concerned, he wasn't.

I got back to Stephen and spoke with him about the feedback I had received from his management. He was genuinely shocked and surprised to learn their views. We agreed that he needed to be more assertive in declaring his successes and that he should embark upon a campaign of unashamed self-promotion. He decided that he should also spend more semi-social time with his management, more lunches (it was the advertising industry after all), more casual discussion and the occasional game of golf. When we finished the conversation he was feeling more positive, considering he had greater clarity on the issues that were stalemating his career, but he was also very apprehensive about his ability to do the things necessary for him to advance.

This all happened about four years ago and through my ongoing association with the agency I have observed with interest Stephen's career progress—or as it turns out, lack of it. Sadly, Stephen has not been able to pull it off. While his more confident and assertive colleagues have gone on to far bigger and better things, he has been shuffled sideways and now fills the role of assistant manager to the position to which he once aspired. His knowledge and experience in the industry is still held in high regard but, as one of his managers so bluntly put it: 'Stephen hasn't got what it takes to be a manager.'

In retrospect it is clear that Stephen lacked the confidence to promote his own abilities.

> ## Be your own political lobbyist—broadcast your successes, wave your own flag.

So exactly how can you build and project your self-confidence in order to develop the positive perceptions of others and to create for yourself a positive political environment?

Believe in yourself

The secret of self-confidence does not lie in your ability to do one or more things particularly well. If you rely on such an ability you will only feel confident while using it, whether it be working, being a support to your manager, making a sale or playing golf. This is the reason that some people become obsessed with certain pursuits and spend all their time involved in one activity to the exclusion of everything else—causing real imbalance in their lives.

True self-confidence exists far deeper than the things you know or do. It is an intrinsic belief in yourself as a person and your ability to succeed. It is your belief in your ability to cope with whatever circumstances life presents, to act decisively when required, to carry on in the face of defeat. It is rooted in a belief and trust in yourself, independent of the consequences of your actions. The value of understanding this concept and living by it, is that, regardless of what life throws your way, despite success or failure, you will always have faith in your own capacity to achieve your goals. Your confidence will not be in your skills and knowledge that are subject to uncontrollable external influence, but rather in your will and determination to learn and to succeed and to do whatever it takes to get where you want to go.

Success cycles

Nevertheless, our levels of confidence are closely linked to our experiences of success and failure. If we are successful at a particular task or challenge we feel positive and confident about ourselves and our abilities generally. This begins a *success cycle*, illustrated in Figure 10:

Figure 10 Success cycle

Ideally we stay in this success cycle continually, building confidence on each success. Unfortunately, life doesn't work that way and our successes are more often than not counterbalanced by negative experiences which may spin us into a *failure cycle*, illustrated in Figure 11:

Figure 11 Failure cycle

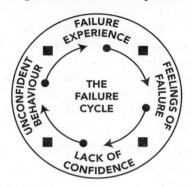

These cycles can explain the 'life attitudes' of some people we meet. People who have a generally positive and successful approach to life focus on their positive and successful experiences even when they are confronted with negative or failure experiences. This enables them to remain in their success cycle and to maintain high levels of confidence. Other people have a negative disposition and tend to focus on their negative and failure experiences, even when they are successful. This locks them into the failure cycle, limiting their success and ensuring low confidence levels. In order to sustain high confidence levels you must attempt to stay locked in your success cycle even when you are faced with failure. You can achieve this by refusing to accept failure as a lifestyle and treating it as a temporary aberration. Realise that you will occasionally spin off into the failure cycle but there is absolutely no reason for you to stay there. Determine to spend little or no time locked into the failure cycle. You can do this by:

- accepting your failures as stepping stones to success
- avoiding self-pity (this self-indulgent trait will keep you in the failure cycle—guaranteed)
- becoming active—do something that will contribute to your next success
- seeing your failure as a learning experience

- focusing on previous success cycles as springboards to your next.

By staying focused on the positive, replaying your successes and treating your failures as learning experiences that will contribute to your next success will sustain your core confidence at a consistently high level.

> ## Stay focused on the positive, replay your successes and treat your failures as learning experiences.

Remove obstacles that exist within

We all possess inner barriers that hinder our confidence and its expression. Even the most apparently confident and self-possessed people have moments of great self-doubt and crises of confidence. Every statesperson, diplomat, politician, celebrity and CEO, if they are honest with themselves, look in the mirror at times and question their right to have achieved the success they have. What they have learned, regardless of the occasional self-doubt, is to remove the psychological obstacles that could potentially hold them back. There is an endless list of reasons people offer for their lack of confidence:

- 'I don't have a proper education.'
- 'I was born on the wrong side of the tracks.'
- 'I've only been here a short time.'
- 'There are a lot of people smarter than I am.'

For every excuse there is a story of someone who has succeeded in the face of similar odds. In order to build your self-confidence and position yourself positively in the eyes of those who matter you will need to remove those internal obstacles that stand in your way.

Five steps to identifying and overcoming obstacles to confidence

1. Identify the things that are causing your lack of confidence.
2. Determine which of these are 'real' and which are only 'perceived'.
3. Of those that are 'real' ask yourself, 'Which of these must I overcome to achieve my goals?'.
4. For those that remain develop a plan to overcome them.
5. Get on with it.

Tools of the trade

There many techniques you can use to help build your confidence. Here is a range of the most effective for your consideration.

Self-talk

Many highly successful sporting personalities use this technique to build their confidence and enhance their performance. Mentally recite positive statements that will reinforce your performance at a particular task. For example, a high jumper facing a jump at a major competition could use statements like:

- 'I can make this jump.'
- 'I have jumped higher than this in training.'
- 'I am jumping better than I have all year.'

Such repeated statements reinforce the positive and are sometimes referred to as 'psyching yourself up' to perform well. Use them when you are:

- about to give an important presentation
- going for a job interview
- writing a report or proposal
- facilitating a meeting.

Self-talk is a technique than can be used when facing any situation where you need to build your confidence levels to ensure a top performance.

Mental imaging

This technique involves running a 'success movie' in your mind—picturing yourself making a perfect performance. It is a powerful tool and one that is extremely easy to use. If you have an important presentation to make before your managers, for example, get yourself comfortable in an easy chair, close your eyes and imagine yourself giving the presentation. Run it through your mind like a movie. Bring the scene down to frame-by-frame detail. See yourself walking into the room, interacting positively with your managers, stepping up to the podium, giving your presentation word by word. Imagine your facial expressions, hand movements, responses from the audience. See yourself changing the overhead transparencies or using the presentation software, referring and talking to each image, making salient points. Picture your audience asking relevant questions and yourself giving clear and meaningful responses. Imagine yourself closing the presentation and receiving positive support and accolades from your managers.

The secret to this technique is imagining the scenario in minute detail and playing it through your mind as a perfect performance. Dr Dennis Waitley, in his book *Seeds of Greatness*,[1] refers to this as 'the power of the imagined experience'. He claims that 'the mind can't tell the difference between an actual experience and an imagined experience that is repeated vividly'. This technique acts like a 'virtual reality' simulation.

Success inventory

We often bury our achievements beneath a moment's negativity. Things can seem so bad that we come out with statements like:

---

1 Dennis Waitley (1983) *Seeds of Greatness*, Brolga Publishing, Victoria, Australia.

- 'I never do anything right.'
- 'I'm hopeless.'
- 'I have to be the world's greatest loser.'

Of course, none of this is true. The circumstances in which you find yourself are so negative that you fail to remember your past successes. A colleague was recently considering moving out of the corporate world to start his own consulting business. I related to some of the things he said, as I had been in the same position not too many years before. His problem was a crisis of confidence.

'I really don't know if I have the skills and ability to do it. Over the last few years I have deskilled significantly, to the point where I feel good for nothing. When consultants come in to talk to me about other issues I am intimidated by their knowledge and experience. Then I wonder how I would succeed competing against them.'

These are all salient points to consider when looking to start you own business, but they must be subject to a severe reality check. My advice to this friend was to conduct a *success inventory* to help put his current thinking into some sort of perspective.

When developing a success inventory put all of the negatives aside and scan your total career history to identify all of the successes you have achieved.

Identify the following:

1. *educational qualifications*—every tertiary course and or training program you have ever completed
2. *individual job roles*—list for each the responsibilities and authority they involved
3. *project involvement*—major successful projects you have been involved in, the skills you used to complete each project and the successful outcomes achieved
4. *major achievements*—a register of your major work achievements and the significance of each.

This information will provide you with a realistic context for analysing your current thinking and making decisions for the future. It will also build your confidence by locking you back into your success cycle.

Projecting confidence

Projecting confidence is the next natural step after building confidence. It is the successful communication to others of your inner conviction of your own abilities and knowledge. Listed below are some techniques that will help you project your confidence.

Be convincing yet flexible

Being confident is not the same as being dogmatic and head-strong. Neither does it require you to be arrogant and conceited. When faced with a situation that demands confidence you need to be convincing but at the same time remain flexible and open to the ideas and suggestions of others.

Being convincing means being able to put forward your perspective with sound and logical arguments, to defend your point of view and reasonably counter any negative comments made. At the same time it is important to remain flexible in your opinions, to consider the suggestions and advice of others and take on board relevant information that could make your ideas even better. The ability to strike a balance between these two stances—conviction and flexibility—will help you avoid seeming arrogant and egotistical.

> **Be strong and stand by your convictions, but don't be given to noble gestures of insignificant impact.**

Stand your ground—know what you know

It is important to be flexible, but projecting confidence also involves being willing to stand your ground when it comes to the crunch. Assertion is not to be mistaken for aggression in these cases—when you know you are right you can afford to state your case with conviction. People who exert this sort of behaviour do so as a matter of principle. Often their knowledge and experience tells them that certain approaches to problems will not work. To state your convictions with passion and ardour when you really know you are right indicates to others a depth of character and commitment to quality.

One word of caution—practising this technique requires skill and balance. Before you make such a stand you must *know* that you are right and, secondly, you must be willing to either walk away or withdraw your support with full knowledge of the consequences. While this is a sure and powerful way to project your confidence it can also backfire dramatically if misused, overused or applied indiscriminately.

Use positive language

The language you use to respond to requests or to answer questions proposed to you can have a significant impact upon how confident you are perceived. Even the way you speak and refer to yourself in everyday conversation can project a lack of confidence. Just as negative self-talk can lower your self-confidence, open self-criticism can lower others' opinions of you. How many times have you heard statements like this:

- 'God, I'm stupid.'
- 'Trust me to make a mistake.'
- 'I'm such a loser.'

After a while you start believing these statements and so do those around you. 'If she thinks she's a loser then she probably knows what she's talking about.'

Negative language such as this emanates from low self-esteem or low self-confidence. This is most evident when people are given a compliment. Often they respond with comments such as:

- 'I didn't do much of the work, I got a lot of help from Christine.'
- 'It was nothing really.'

- 'Yeah, it's nice, but it's not such a big deal. I bought it on sale.'

Consciously take control of the language you use on an everyday basis. Agree to never belittle yourself or put yourself down in front of others. Determine to use positive language even when faced with negative situations:

- 'I don't know how that happened. I'll find out and make sure it doesn't happen again.'
- 'Let's fix it then.'
- 'I am certain it was a random error—I'll make sure it is.'

There are enough people in life who are willing to point out your mistakes and emphasise the negative things you do. Make sure you are not one of them.

My great-grandmother gave me some advice when she was in her 90s regarding the acceptance of compliments: 'There are only ever two words to say when someone gives you a compliment—"thank you". Anything more is pretension, anything less displays a lack of self-worth.' This has been extremely sound advice.

Just remember that people will think of you as you tell them to think—it's up to you to ensure they think of you well.

> **There are only ever two words to say when someone gives you a compliment: Thank you.**

Credibility and trust

Credibility and trust are the outcomes or end products of a long string of consistent behaviours and actions, rather than skills or techniques that can be developed or learned.

61

Developing a reputation for competence and confidence at work will take you a long way to earning the credibility and trust of your management and peers. There are, however, a number of guiding principles you should embrace to ensure that you achieve the highest levels of credibility and trust at work.

Why bother?

Good question, and one that deserves an answer. Remember, positive politics is all about the interaction of individuals to achieve common goals; it's about relationships and people influencing each other in an environment where both individual and organisational goals are being met. In this environment, credibility and trust act as the oil that makes the political machine run smoothly. Due to the informal nature of political environments, agreements and decisions that are made rarely involve any formal documentation. Simply put, if people don't trust you then they won't co-operate and it becomes impossible to develop win/win/win strategies. If you lack credibility then your managers and peers will not want to be involved with you in any activity that could threaten their reputation or make them look bad. Credibility and trust are the essence of creating a positive political environment.

Credibility means to be 'worthy of belief' or 'trustworthy', and to trust means 'to have confidence in' or 'to believe'. In the context of positive politics credibility and trust involves:

developing relationships in your work environment where those you work with believe in your ability to deliver, consider you to be trustworthy and know that your motives are for the common good of the organisation and the individuals involved.

It is important to realise that credibility and trust are qualities that can't be demanded of others. These qualities must be earned through consistent and honest dealings. And even once earned, they can easily be lost—one dishonest dealing or selfish act can ruin years of effort. Credibility and trust, once gained, must be carefully guarded and protected.

Christine

Christine Johnson was the managing director of a software distribution company that had been extremely successful in its eight years of operation, having developed a high profile in a very competitive industry. Projected growth for the company in the next financial year was very positive and plans to take on new product and expand their distribution network had been enthusiastically received by the board of shareholders. Christine's style of management encouraged high levels of loyalty and commitment from her employees. The company had developed a 'family' atmosphere and the employees often went above and beyond the call of duty in order to meet their customers' needs.

Early in 1995, Christine was called to a special board meeting where it was announced that two of the key shareholders intended to sell their stock to one buyer that would give that buyer the major shareholding. In order to make the business seem as attractive to the prospective buyer as possible, Christine was asked to reduce staff levels by 15 people. Initially she put up a fight, declaring the need for all of her staff in order to meet projected targets for the next financial year, but she soon realised that any argument would be in vain and reluctantly agreed to meet their demands by the end of the month.

On returning to her office she immediately called her five department managers into a meeting where she explained the situation and sought their input on how they should go about such an onerous task. They agreed that the decision on who should be retrenched would be determined by identifying those areas that could best sustain the loss. A list of 15 names containing people who had been with the company since its inception was painfully drawn up. Next, the team discussed how these people should be advised of their retrenchment. Each manager volunteered to break the bad news to their respective employees and the meeting was concluded. As a very sober management team started to disperse, Christine cut across their deliberations on the unpleasant task ahead:

'I don't feel comfortable about this!'

'Well, Christine, I don't think any of us really do,' Warren Klein from marketing responded.

'No, I mean that I am not sure that you as managers should be breaking this news. As awkward as it may be, I think I should do it.'

Each of the managers looked at each other.

'None of us are going to argue with you on that one, Christine.' Amanda Gardener from production had already started contemplating the meetings she would have and her stomach was churning.

'Let's set up the meetings and I will talk to each person individually with you present.'

The meetings did not go particularly well. Christine explained the situation to each person and went to great lengths to point out that their retrenchment had nothing to do with their performance. She was open and honest with information and answered any questions that were asked frankly and with directness. The reactions ranged from tears to anger but by the end of the exercise each person expressed their gratitude for how the situation had been handled and the value they had derived from working for the company. Later that day Christine addressed the entire company and explained the situation and the regret of the management team and the shareholders that this situation existed.

With time the transfer of the company's ownership took place and the new directors encouraged the pursuit of the original growth strategies proposed in the business plan. The company continued to grow on schedule and within six months they were looking to employ more staff. Christine personally contacted all of the 15 people she had had to retrench six months previously and asked if they would consider rejoining the company in their previous positions. To her astonishment, every one of them agreed, even though some of them had secured 'better' positions.

In this case, Christine had established a long-standing reserve of credibility and trust with her staff. She handled an awkward situation with openness, honesty and integrity. The fact that she chose to announce the bad news herself earned her huge amounts of respect and admiration. This was proven in the end by the people she had retrenched wanting to come back and work for her.

Guiding principles for developing credibility and trust

Credibility and trust are not skills that you can learn, however, there are a number of guiding principles you can apply to help their development.

Listen to understand

Creating a positive political environment demands the development of joint goals. To this end, it is important to learn to listen effectively. When dealing with others you should seek to understand what their goals are, listen empathically, probe and pursue clarity around what it is they are trying to achieve. See the situation from their perspective and consider objectives. In this way, you can identify areas for synergy and co-operation, and endeavour to develop strategies that will ensure that all parties win.

Show common courtesy

Nothing can replace common courtesy and respect for developing credibility and trust. While you may clash actively over work issues, there is no excuse for being anything less than civil in all circumstances. Common courtesy involves being kind, friendly and thoughtful, showing regard for people's feelings and extending to them politeness and consideration regardless of the circumstances. For those that live by the 'eye for an eye' rule this will be a difficult task— but this rule is the keystone of negative politics. An old Jewish proverb suggests that treating your enemies with kindness and respect 'heaps coals of fire on their heads' meaning that

65

it will make them angry and confused and cause any act of revenge on their part to be fruitless. Though you might find this strategy a bit much, don't allow those who oppose you to drag you down to their level of poor behaviour.

Avoid argument

The simple adage 'no one wins an argument' is one that should be kept in mind when in the workplace. It is often tempting to go head to head with someone, particularly when you know you are right or have the authority to pull rank on them. Even if you get the upper hand in an argument, you are usually left with bad feelings and contempt between the warring parties. Sound advice when faced with a potential argument is to *walk away* rather than be confrontational. Developing a reputation for being argumentative and confrontational makes it much harder for you to develop collaborative relationships.

Be honest and open

Strive at all times to be honest and open. Usually the prevailing culture within organisations is to be secretive and restrictive with the information you share. People are very sensitive to this sort of behaviour and if they perceive that you are hiding something they will be reluctant to trust you or co-operate in any way—and with just cause. In all your dealings with people play it straight, don't have hidden agendas, let them know what you want to get out of your collaboration. To some degree it is important to be vulnerable. Express your fears and doubts, tell them you don't know if 'it' will work, seek their advice and input, be willing to incorporate their ideas. This will encourage them to trust you and to be open and honest themselves.

Be gracious in the acceptance of criticism

A manager I once worked with used this throwaway line: 'Her problem is she can't take criticism!'. Fact is, few of us can. What we do or propose, we own. If someone chooses to criticise our actions or behaviours then we are very likely to take it personally. Indeed, we often respond so badly to criticism (by becoming defensive or, worse, going into denial) we fail to identify any good in what our critic is saying. We must learn the hard lesson that there may actually be some value in criticism. Be gracious, listen to what they say and determine if there is anything valuable to extract from their comments. And if you do take their advice, let them know about it.

Accept diversity

One of the benefits of working with a wide range of different people is the opportunity to be exposed to a multiplicity of ideas and divergent approaches to situations and problems. Those who are narrowminded cannot see the benefit of seeking the ideas and input of others. If you are to create a positive political environment you must accept and even celebrate the diversity of those with whom you work, with the view of learning from the variety of their backgrounds and experience. A healthy respect for the individual and a sincere recognition of the value of their contribution will not only endear you to them but will enrich your work and efforts.

Avoid duplicity

Being referred to as 'two-faced' is not a pleasant accolade and one that should be avoided at all costs. Duplicity involves saying one thing to one person and something contradictory to another or saying things about others that may or may not be true yet puts them in a negative light. Adopt the principle of not saying anything about someone that you would not honestly say to their face. Be loyal to your colleagues and friends; don't purposely undermine others or put them down; defend those that are being maligned. This is starting to sound like a sermon, I know, but the principles are sound and advisable if you truly seek to build credibility and trust. If people find out that you are saying unpleasant things about them behind their back, they will never trust you.

67

Now to begin . . .

This chapter has focused on the foundations that must be laid before you can build a positive political environment. In many cases you will already be practising many of these techniques and have developed these important skills. But it is vital that you get these basics right before you try anything else.

In Chapter 3 we will explore the many different ways of building your reputation and ensuring you are being noticed around the office—for all the right reasons.

Chapter 3

BUILDING YOUR REPUTATION

GET NOTICED FOR ALL THE RIGHT REASONS

'If one's reputation is a possession, then of all my possessions, my reputation means most to me.'

Arthur Ashe

Constantly we judge others and are ourselves judged upon our reputations.

'Does anyone know a good plumber?'

'Yeah, I do. His name is Colin. He's a bit slow in the mornings but warms up after a couple of cups of coffee. Did a great job on my place.'

We prefer to deal with people who have been recommended to us based upon the experiences of someone else. Even if the information about the person is secondhand it is better than having to deal with someone we know absolutely nothing about. When you ask someone how they generate business and they say 'word of mouth', what they are actually saying is, 'I trade off my good reputation.' They have developed a reputation of some standing in their area of expertise and people are willing to tell others about their experiences.

Rachel and Mike

'Rachel, thanks for calling back. I just wanted to get your input. Yesterday I interviewed a guy for a training and development position. His name is Miles Green. He says he used to work for your organisation and I thought you may have come across him.'

There was a slight pause on the other end of the line. Rachel was gathering her thoughts and considering her answer.

'Yes, I remember him well. He did some work in our area about 12 months ago. What do you want to know?'

'Really I just wanted to get some general feedback from you on the stamp of the guy and whether you think he would fit in over here.'

There was another slight pause.

'Is this conversation "on" or "off" the record?'

'Off the record—totally.'

'Between you and I, you would be crazy to touch him with a 40-foot barge pole. Let me tell you why. You know our company is reasonably small and as the most senior female executive here a lot of the women feel comfortable to come and talk to me. During the 18 months Miles was with us, I had five women come and talk to me about pressing sexual harassment charges against him. None did, by the way. He never did anything that was "chargeable" *per se*, he was just sleazy and suggestive. I think it all got a bit hot for him and he moved on. After he left, I heard similar stories from people I know in other organisations.'

'Was it really as bad as people have made out though, Rachel? Often these things are blown out of proportion.'

Rachel took a deep breath.

'Mike, who really knows? You asked, I told. Fact is, he developed a bad reputation for himself. Perception or reality—frankly it doesn't matter in my books. "Where there's smoke there's fire." For a person like him in a responsible training role, you can't afford to be sending out the wrong signals.'

'So you think I could end up with a sexual harassment case on my hands with this one?'

'He could have changed, turned over a new leaf, found Jesus or Buddha. All I can tell you is my experiences with him in the past—and they weren't good.'

'Rachel, thanks very much for that. As good as he

seems, the last thing I need is that sort of trouble. Whose turn is it to shout lunch?'

'If it was mine, it's yours now. I might have just saved you a lot of money.'

Reputation—whether you like it or not you have one. You are building one for yourself every day. The things you do, the way you behave, react and interact, the way you communicate, your level of competence, your interpersonal effectiveness and many other factors are all compounding to develop your reputation. Regardless of the business or profession you are in, everyone is a salesperson. You are selling yourself in some way, developing your reputation. People believe what they see, they absorb the things they observe and draw conclusions over time based on the consistent (or inconsistent) messages they receive. The main question is, are you conscious of the reputation you are building—do you have a strategy, a plan that you are working to, are you in control? The probable answer to these questions is—no! That doesn't necessarily mean you are creating a bad reputation for yourself, but it does mean you could be far more effective than you are currently.

The quality of your reputation is closely linked to the political influence you bring to bear in your work environment. A strong, positive reputation establishes your credibility and generates an aura of competence, reliability and trust. A poor reputation undermines your efforts to influence. People remember past behaviours of inconsistency and less than adequate performance and align those with future performance—in most cases, rightly so. It is extremely hard to re-establish a reputation that has been ruined or tarnished. Images and experiences stick in people's minds long after logic and reason suggest things will have changed. Consequently, it is wise to keep the development of your reputation at the front of mind so you never find yourself in a situation where you could ruin it and undermine your ability to influence.

This chapter looks at some of the major factors that combine to generate the signals and messages that make up your reputation. This information will provide you with the means to develop a strategy for enhancing your reputation and controlling the ways people perceive you. As you move through your career creating and shaping your political environment, your reputation will be your currency of trade.

What is reputation?

A reputation is:

> what is generally said or believed about a person's or thing's character; state of being well reported of, credit, distinction, respectability, good fame.
>
> *Concise Oxford Dictionary*

In most cases, our reputations are built brick by tedious brick. Millions of conversations and interactions, as well as the things said about us by others every day, combine to create the reputation's rather delicate fabric. There are sometimes one-off events that can quickly establish a reputation— the person who runs into a burning building to save a child immediately gets a reputation as a hero. They acquire the characteristics of courage, bravery and selflessness through one act, developing a reputation that might otherwise take years to establish. Such situations are rare, particularly in the work environment. Unfortunately, most of us are stuck with the 'day by day, step by step, inch by burdensome inch' method of developing our reputation.

The irony is that having taken so long to build a positive reputation it is so easily lost. One act of indiscretion at the Christmas party can bring it tumbling down, and extricating yourself from the implications of a reputation that has collapsed can take years.

Within an organisation there is such a thing as 'reputational capital'. It is the credit you build in your personal account that will hold you in good stead if you need to draw on it when faced with a political situation. Consider the following situation.

Joy

Joy Tanner was a bit of an institution in her organisation. Smith and Co were manufacturers of shoes and Joy had started with them in their first year of operation, 23 years ago. She started as a packer on the production line and was now a frontline supervisor, not because she didn't have the talent to go further, but in her own words, 'I'm one of the workers. Always have been, always will be. That's where I belong.' Joy loved mixing it with the staff and over the years had formed some very loyal and lasting friendships with her workmates. She was respected as being a 'firm but fair' supervisor that called a spade a spade and was as honest as the day. She was reliable and trustworthy—one of those people you can really depend upon to stand by you when things go wrong. On many occasions over the years, particularly in the early days, she had stood shoulder to shoulder with the owners late in the night to get a special order completed to deadline.

'Just part of the job,' she would say, but it was these acts of commitment that made Joy the person she was, and an incredible asset to the company.

An incident occurred between Joy and another supervisor, Linda. While Linda was ambitious and took every opportunity to push her case with management, she was less than capable and sought to manipulate and control her staff rather than work with them as a team. Before anyone was promoted to a position above supervisor, Joy was consulted and asked her opinion. When asked about Linda, she gave her typical frank and honest appraisal of the way she interacted with her staff: 'Her people skills are pathetic.' Management decided to promote someone else. Linda was peeved. She knew Joy was the person who had hindered her progress and she was determined to get revenge.

Mysteriously, things started going missing around the factory. First it was a couple of pairs of shoes that disappeared, then a CD someone had brought in to listen to on their portable player. Over two or three weeks it became obvious that one of the staff was stealing things regularly. Management spoke to everyone and told them to be careful of their personal things and to pass on any information if it came to hand. There was a lot of gossip around the factory as to who might be the offender, but no one really knew.

It all came to a head when Molly went to her locker on Thursday afternoon to find it had been prised open and her weekly salary stolen. Management called in the police and for few days things were extremely tense. Then management received an anonymous, typed note advising them that Joy had been observed acting suspiciously and going into the ladies' locker room on the day of the crime.

Rhonda, the factory manager, called Joy into her office and closed the door.

'Joy, we've received a letter.'

The note was encased in a plastic bag. She pushed it across the desk so Joy could read it.

'What do you think, Rhonda?' Joy asked after reading it.

'I think someone is trying to set you up.'

'Could be true, of course,' Joy prodded.

Rhonda smiled.

'Joy, you were my boss when I started here 15 years ago. During that time I have never seen you lift a finger to do anything that hurt either the company or anyone who works here. You know what Michael Smith did when I showed him this? He laughed. Not just a chuckle, I mean he really laughed. So did I. It is so ridiculous to think you would do what is suggested in this letter . . .'

They both smiled.

'Where to from here?' Joy asked.

'Just sit tight. We think we are about to catch the culprit.'

Sure enough, two days later Linda was caught red-handed rifling through someone's handbag. When the police searched her locker they also found the pay slip from the stolen wages. The case was closed and Linda was relieved of her duties.

In this situation Joy's reputation for honesty and integrity was so strong that those who were faced with questioning her found it impossible even to imagine her responsible for the theft. Her reputational capital was so great that this situation did not even make a dent in the deposits she had made over the years. *That* is the type of reputation we all need.

If you develop a reputation for thorough and detailed work you hold that to your credit: 'I know Richard is really pushing to get this project, even to the point where he is rubbishing Shu's work, but I really think Shu has the track record that suggests he is the best person for the job.' For 'track record' read 'reputation'.

If you have a reputation for accurately forecasting situations, that will be held in your favour until it is required—'Wendel thinks that the market will slow within the next month, but Cheryl believes the current situation will hold at least until Christmas. We are yet to see Cheryl's predictions proved wrong, so I think we should run with her proposal.'

Reputational capital is a commodity you can trade every day, and is often traded on your behalf and without your consent by people in positions to influence your career. This being the case, you must give them plenty of capital to play with and allow them the opportunity to spend it freely on your account—don't ever let people run out of good things to say about you. A professional reputation is an essential tool for creating a positive political environment.

Was that a perception or a reality?

Have you ever been faced with a situation where perception clashes with reality? Recently I conducted an attitude survey for a client to determine some of the key issues the staff believed the company was facing. One of the unpleasant things I had to tell the managing director was staff's perception that she was directive and dictatorial in her management style. *'But I try to involve the staff as often as I can in making important decisions. I delegate responsibility, I run team meetings. What else do they want me to do?'*

75

Understandably she was very defensive. However, I had to convince her that regardless of the positive things she felt she was doing as a manager, the perception of her staff was still that she had a directive and dictatorial management style. For them, perception was reality and if she was going to effectively implement change she had to accept this and work to change the existing perception.

In an ideal world, perception and reality would be the same things. That is, the way we perceive things to be would in fact be the way they really are. However, there will almost always be a gap, regardless of how small, between what we believe is the truth and the actual truth.

Reality deals with logic and fact, while perception deals with a mix of logic, fact, emotions, feelings and personal interpretations and experience. It is no wonder that often one person's perception is so different from another's. Have you ever been in a situation where someone has said, 'Isn't Bill a great guy?', only for someone else to turn around and say 'I think he is an absolute fool.'?

Perception is what our *mind* sees, not what our eye sees. And what the mind sees is not based on logic and fact alone. I read an article in the newspaper recently about a boy of 16 who passed himself off as a government agent for 18 months, soliciting information, opening bank accounts, securing credit, travelling the country, staying in plush hotels and even donating thousands of dollars of government money to charity. How? By developing the perception he was someone other than who he really was.

A distinguished older woman walks into a jewellery store. She is well dressed, conservative, well spoken, casual and relaxed as she looks at the very expensive jewellery on display. The owner watches her out of the corner of his eye but is not too concerned with what he sees—no security risk here. Eventually she asks to see some bracelets and rings. She is extremely pleasant and 'normal' for a woman of her class and standing. She takes her time, she is in no hurry, other customers come and go. When the owner returns to attend to her she has gone, and so has a range of his jewellery. His perceptions told him that he had nothing to worry about with this woman. Reality was she travelled the world projecting this image and stealing hundreds of thousands of dollars worth of jewellery a year.

What our mind sees is often not what we get. How can we make this situation work for us in our political work environments?

There is a common saying among salespeople: 'Fake it till you make it'. It suggests that if you are not yet a top-flight salesperson you should act as if you are. When it comes to building for yourself a professional reputation, and through your reputation exerting political influence, the same principle applies. Once you have determined the reputation that will give you the best political advantage, such as 'cool under pressure' or 'able to get the job done', start projecting this behaviour, even if you don't feel that way inside. Internally you may be about to explode or burst into tears, but externally you are calm and controlled, projecting confidence and capability. Those around you will develop their perceptions based only on what they see and interpret through their 'mind's eye'. If you are consistent with such projections you will eventually get a reputation for being calm in high pressure situations or capable of getting results.

What reputation do you want to develop? What characteristics do you want to be recognised for? Start projecting those qualities now. *Fake it till you make it*. People will perceive you as having these qualities and eventually, you will actually develop them.

Concentrating on these areas and consciously projecting predetermined behaviours will quickly build and alter the perceptions held by those people you need to affect.

Let's look at some of the key factors that combine to create your reputation.

Professional image

As with reputation, everyone has a professional image whether they like it or not, and it is important to ensure you manage and control yours—don't let it develop by accident.

77

There is a range of things you should consider that will raise the perception of your professionalism in the work environment. Think about developing the following attitudes in your quest for a professional image.

Quality

Always aim to produce work of the highest quality. What is quality? With the introduction of the quality revolution many organisations have implemented quality standards and processes. In line with quality assurance principles, quality is:

- a philosophy that focuses on continuous improvement
- doing it right the first time
- working within guidelines
- conforming to set standards, processes and procedures.

By always meeting and, when possible, exceeding the standards set by your organisation you will develop the perception of a person who produces high quality work.

Currency

Would you like to be operated on by a surgeon who graduated in 1947 and hasn't picked up a book or learned anything since? No, neither would I. Staying current in the area of your expertise and keeping abreast of the latest trends is a critical factor in retaining a professional image. The best way to do this is by subscribing to professional journals, attending industry seminars, registering on list servers on the Internet or going along to professional evenings organised by industry bodies. It does take time and effort but it is far better than the alternative—being known as a dinosaur.

Continual learning

Adopting an attitude of continual learning is an adjunct to remaining current. Have you ever heard the old question, 'Has he got 10 years' experience or one year's experience 10 times?'. Some people get offended when they find out that there is something they don't know. They take even more offence when they find out someone younger or less experienced can teach them something. By retaining an open mind and learning from whomever you can, whenever you can, you will retain a professional image that is aligned with modern practice. Add to your knowledge by continuing to study, reading new books and attending training programs. I was told at a function one evening by a lady in her 60s who was studying for her HSC that 'life is a learning experience'—who was I to argue?

Goal setting

True professionals don't wander through their careers, they set goals for themselves and commit to achieving them. By the time you finish this book you will have uncovered a wide range of areas in which you can set yourself goals to improve your political work environment. You will also have the means by which to develop a long-term strategy for success in this area. Do it—don't just wander through your career and hope it will happen. People who set goals and achieve them have an aura of success. The image they project is one that says, 'anything is possible'; 'tell me what it is we need to achieve and we'll do it'.

Classic attitudes

There are also a range of what we could call 'classic attitudes' that, if practised, will guarantee a professional image and reputation.

> **Be a positive person rather than one who is always critical or negative. Don't bring your manager problems, bring solutions.**

79

Have a positive attitude

Train yourself to always view things from a positive perspective. Always look for the good in an idea, suggestion or person. When you have exhausted the positives, then think about the negatives. Get a reputation for being a positive person rather than the one who is always critical or negative. Don't bring your manager problems, bring solutions.

Adopt a sound work ethic

In some organisations I have worked with there is a prevailing work ethic that suggests it is the role of the employee to do as little as possible and to take the company for all you can get. It you adopt a 'giving' rather than a 'taking' mentality towards your work you will develop a reputation as a person who is willing to put in effort to get the job done, someone who will go the extra mile. People with this sort of reputation are the ones who can exert the most influence when it really matters—an important and valuable advantage in a political situation.

Use your initiative

I'm sure you have heard managers say that enough times. What it really means is, 'I have too many other things to think about, work it out for yourself'. If you can do a task efficiently don't ask for help. If you see something that needs to be done, do it. You don't need to seek permission. If you take this approach you will become invaluable to your manager. Stay one step ahead, do things before you are asked. It is a great feeling, when your boss says 'Could you please do . . .' to be able to say 'I have already done that, I have it here'.

Be a team player

Especially in today's work environment, where teams are an important part of organisational structure, it is crucial to be seen as a team player. Get a reputation for being easy to get along with, co-operative, supportive, helpful and friendly.

Be careful not to isolate people or to be seen as a 'loner'. This doesn't mean you can't have an opinion or that you can't be assertive—quite the opposite. It does mean that if you are going to assert your opinion you should be aware of and consider other people's viewpoints.

Be responsible and accountable

There are many people in organisations who are only too ready to duck the issue or pass the blame onto someone else. Develop a reputation for playing it straight and facing up to situations where you might have stuffed up. Be willing to take the blame yourself; never be tempted to try and pass it on to someone else. If you are managing a team of people be careful not to suggest it was their fault—even if it was. You are responsible for the team and therefore you should take the rap. This also means you get to accept the accolades when things go right. However, if you are managing a team in this situation you are better served by passing the praise on—you may need the team's help next time.

Exercise self-control

It is vital that you learn to control your emotions, as lack of self-control indicates immaturity and often insecurity. People who can't control their temper and lash out at anyone or anything within reach lose respect and credibility among management, peers and staff. Those who cry under pressure, lash out verbally, or say things that are hurtful or unwarranted are considered unstable and often treated with caution. Such behaviour also indicates a lack of respect for others. It might feel good at the time but it will give you a poor reputation in the long run.

You professional image is the single tool that will give you greatest critical leverage when you are faced with a political situation that requires significant influence. It is your reputation for professionalism that will make people feel confident and comfortable about you doing the job, so it needs to be guarded, nurtured and nourished to ensure you maximise its value.

81

Dean and June

Over the past five years Dean had developed a reputation as a professional in his field that was recognised at the most senior levels of the organisation. He always gave requests that were generated from the executive floor the highest priority. He was thorough in his work and presented ideas and solutions that were current, workable and suited the culture of the organisation. Dean worked hard to achieve his goals; he was a team player who held the organisation's benefit firmly in mind and used his initiative to advance his agendas as quickly as possible within the normal constraints of departmental management. The relationships he had developed with his peers were professional rather than social, he was seen as focused and determined, yet friendly, co-operative and personable—unless you deliberately crossed him or took him for granted, when it could get ugly. Generally, Dean was a valuable employee who successfully got results.

When June joined the company her role overlapped significantly with Dean's. Where Dean was personable and co-operative, June was aggressive, with something to prove. She was a young woman in a hurry who didn't really care for the people she thought stood in her way. It didn't take long for June to develop a reputation as being extremely capable but very difficult to manage. Dean and June clashed right from the start. June expected Dean to capitulate to her ideas and strategies from the very beginning, regardless of the fact that his insight into the organisation's culture suggested those ideas would encounter major problems. After only a short time the tension between them precluded any constructive collaboration.

Things came to a head when June strongly disagreed with a product development strategy Dean and his team had created with a senior product manager. She decided to go over Dean's head and called a meeting between the senior product manager and the managing director to point out where the strategy was flawed.

After June had put forward her case the managing

director asked a few pertinent questions then turned to the senior product manager.

'Michelle, what are your views on what June has to say?'

'I can see her point regarding advertising expenditure and the relative scheduling, however, my view is that these are a matter of preference rather than relevance. In the course of the product's development I believe either approach will work. The point is that I have worked with Dean on a number of similar strategies and have found his approach to be both sound and successful. While I appreciate June's input, I am far more inclined at this point to take Dean's advice based on his past track record.'

The MD was watching June closely to fathom her reaction. He could see that she was beginning to become agitated and uncomfortable with the direction in which the meeting was headed.

'But that's the very point I am trying to make, Michelle. Dean's approaches are antiquated—he's a bit of a dinosaur really . . .'

Before June's dialogue deteriorated into further character assassination, the MD cut her off sharply.

'Thank you, June. Michelle, it sounds like you are confident of the strategy you have developed with Dean?'

'Absolutely.'

'Then we really don't have anything else to discuss. Thank you, Michelle. June, would you mind staying a moment? We need to talk.'

Michelle exited the room quickly. She had seen the MD in such a mood before—he was loading his guns.

'June, you are new to this company and I will allow you one indiscretion on that account. However, I want to make it clear to you that I will not tolerate that sort of behaviour at your level of management. Dean has worked for this organisation for five years now. During that time he has proven himself to be a capable and committed professional. As managing director, I have personally benefited from his insights and on occasion sought his opinion on a number of important matters. His standing in this organisation is extremely high for no other reason than he consistently does very good work in a very professional manner. I will not have you, who have yet to prove to me your worth, undermine Dean's professional standing in my or anyone else's presence. Do I make myself clear?'

There was a slight pause and an indignant reply.

'Yes.'

June left the meeting wondering how on earth she had miscalculated so badly the strength of Dean's standing with executive management. She couldn't work out what they saw in him.

Faced with a political situation that was completely out of his control, all Dean had to depend upon was his reputation. Dean may have remained blissfully unaware of this meeting and the fact that the success of his strategy was on the line. However, while he was going about his business, conversations were being conducted and decisions being made that drew upon the reputational capital he had deposited over the five years he had worked for the organisation. When it was most crucial, his reputation spoke for him even in his absence.

Communication

The way we communicate can have a significant bearing on the development of our reputation. Our communication style sends out messages about us: how we think; how well organised we are; where our values lie; the respect we have for others. People pick up on these messages and from them form assumptions and opinions. Once again, there is great value in actually controlling the messages we send out in order to create the reputation we want for ourselves.

There are three basic ways of communicating in the workplace that combine to influence your reputation, and a balanced capability in all three areas is necessary to maximise your impact:

1. one-on-one
2. written
3. presentations.

One-on-one

One-on-one communication with an individual is a complex skill as it embraces a range of visual components such as body language, eye contact and facial expressions. When these are combined with the words and the way they are being said you have a large number of stimuli that join to send and reinforce your message. When these are all focused and in sync they can have an extremely high impact on the individual receiving your message. Every time you meet with someone it is an opportunity to reinforce the image and reputation you are trying to project. There are a number of basic things you can do to ensure you make the most of every occasion:

Give a firm handshake
There is nothing worse than a 'wet fish' handshake. It communicates a lack of self-confidence and strength of character. Right or wrong, it is certainly the message it sends. Ensure your handshake is firm and confident without being a 'bonebreaker'. This applies to women just as much as it does to men.

Make eye contact
By looking someone in the eye you are communicating a healthy self-image as well as openness and honesty.

Be confident
Know what you are talking about, appreciate your own worth and refuse to be intimidated.

Listen actively
Respond while the person you are talking to is speaking— show them you are interested and comprehending by nodding your head, saying 'I see' or 'ah hah'.

85

Feedback information

Show you understand what is being said by using the feedback technique. At an appropriate time in the conversation say, 'So what you are saying is . . .' or 'You mean . . .'. This confirms what is being said and your level of understanding. If there is a need for clarity, the other person can repeat what they have said.

Set objectives

Before every meeting you attend, take the time to establish for yourself the objectives you wish to achieve. Ask 'What do I want to get out of this meeting?'. Make sure you are prepared and have all of the appropriate materials and documentation.

These techniques will reinforce the fact that you are a professional person to deal with, and you know what you are talking about.

Make the most of every one-on-one communication to confirm your reputation.

Confession of a tough management decision

Ryan could be described as just 'left of centre' when it came to his appearance. It wasn't that he dressed particularly badly, it was more the combination of what he wore. For example, he always wore a suit and tie to work, but not always matching pants and jacket—it was the combination of checks and stripes that looked the worst. Shirts of strong colours with clashing ties, inappropriate socks and pants just a little too short. Ryan always looked like he had just stepped out of a tumble drier. Just a bit scruffy, wrinkled and frayed around the edges. None of this had anything whatsoever to do with his work. He was very good at what he did and in most cases excelled beyond his peers.

When we had to consider who to promote into the new management position we really struggled. Ryan had the goods technically but his appearance made him seem disorganised, a bit careless and scatty—which he wasn't.

People found it hard to take him seriously because he was 'different', even eccentric, in his dress. The other candidate for the job didn't have quite as much experience, but the image they presented was very sound and professional. We thought that this would make a better impression on the staff and give them a role model that was more in line with the organisation's image and culture. This was an important feature of this new role, as the person selected would be representing the company on a range of external committees.

It's a shame about Ryan, he has a lot of potential—if only he could scrub up a bit.

Written presentation

Your written communication is also a means of sending messages that can reinforce your reputation. Recently I received a letter addressed 'Dear Madam'. The fact that I am male seemed to have totally escaped the organisation—no doubt the letter came from a mass mailing list. Still, this is no excuse. It communicated to me that the company did not pay attention to detail. I could not take their product seriously after such an error.

Your written communication can convey similar messages. If you want a reputation for being accurate, well organised and reliable then you must become fastidious about every piece of communication that leaves your desk with your name on it. This applies even to email messages, where there is a general tendency to be extremely sloppy. Don't fall into the trap of compromising your standards—it's your reputation.

There are just a few rules that you should adhere to:

Spelling
Read and re-read your letters and documents to ensure the spelling is correct. Don't rely solely on the spellcheck function of your computer as it will not pick up words that are spelled incorrectly for a particular context. For example, the bane of my life is the word *from*. For some reason, my fingers only want to type *form*. Of course, *form* is a word the

spellchecker quite rightly accepts. Make sure *you* check your work.

Grammar

Some are good at grammar, others are pretty ordinary and still others are terrible. If you know you have a problem, get someone else to check your written work for you. I tutored a postgrad course for a while and a couple of the first assignments handed in were grammatical disasters. After the shock of the marks they received, and a bit of advice on the side, two of the students started to get help with their grammar. At least, I think they did, because I never had a problem with their work after that one incident. Brilliant ideas can be lost behind the fog of poor grammar.

Layout

You may think this is petty, however, the way you present your letters and documents can send very loud messages. If they are haphazard and confusing, the person trying to read them may not get the essence of what you are trying to say. It could also be construed that this—haphazard and confused—is the way you think. On the other hand, a document that is well presented, easy to read and flows nicely communicates order and control to the reader. The appropriate use of bold headings, bullet points, indents and so forth, can really enhance the message a document is trying to communicate.

The general advice regarding all written material you are responsible for is—be fussy. Be pedantic, don't let a report containing bad spelling weaken your effectiveness or jeopardise your political influence.

Presentations

The final area of communication that has a significant impact on your reputation is public presentations. When you must speak to a group of people you are provided with a fabulous opportunity to enhance your reputation rapidly. Of course, the opposite is true if you do a disastrous job. Many people have a complete phobia about speaking in public. Quite a few years ago I was conducting a public presentation course for a group of senior managers. One of the group was the Sales and Marketing Director for a sizeable company and before she had to give her first short presentation to the group she came up to me and said, 'Look, I thought you should know I am a little nervous about having to do this.' Considering that giving presentations was the whole purpose of the course, I strongly encouraged her to participate and eventually she agreed. When it came her turn to speak, she walked shakily up to the podium and said 'Hi, I'm going to talk . . .' and froze solid.

I had read about people to whom this had happened, but had never seen it firsthand. We all waited for her to say something else, but she didn't. There she stood, mid-sentence, hand poised, not moving. Eventually I had to get up, take her by the arm and lead her back to her seat.

You can appreciate that having this type of problem while presenting to the board would not be particularly positive for your reputation. On the other hand I have seen many a person benefit greatly from putting a lot of effort, though they may not have felt terribly enthusiastic about doing it, into their presentations. It is an invaluable opportunity to 'strut your stuff'—to confirm to people how good you are and influence a group of people rather than just one-on-one.

Here is some simple advice on how to maximise your presentation opportunities:

- Don't avoid opportunities to speak to groups. Search out these opportunities and speak as often as possible.
- Always prepare adequately. Don't be tempted to prepare on the run. It is too important an opportunity to do badly.
- Ensure your presentation is correctly structured. If you haven't done a presentation skills or public speaking course, sign up for one immediately.
- Never, ever read a presentation. It is boring, uninteresting and robs you of any ability to build rapport with your audience through eye contact.

- Use visuals if you can. Overheads, slides or computer projected images can add lots of colour and interest to your presentation.
- Know your audience and direct your presentation appropriately.
- Speak clearly and evenly—don't rush what you have to say.
- Know your material well and be prepared to answer questions.

Giving public presentation is one of the best means by which you can either enhance or ruin your reputation. If you are going to give a presentation, do it properly, do it well. It is really worth the effort.

Personal image

Professor Albert Mehrabian of UCLA[2] conducted research involving the three major components that combine in the communication of a message—the verbal, vocal and visual. His research concluded that these three components combine to develop trust, believability and impact during communication.

The three components are:

1. *verbal*—that is, the actual words we say, the message itself
2. *vocal*—that is, the way we say it, intonation, emphasis, projection
3. *visual*—that is, the things people see, facial expression, movement, dress.

Mehrabian's research found that in the development of trust and believability each of the components were responsible for different amounts of the final impression received, as illustrated in Figure 12.

---

2 Albert Mehrabian (1981) *Silent Messages*, Wordsworth Publishing Co., Belmont, CA.

Figure 12 The development of believability

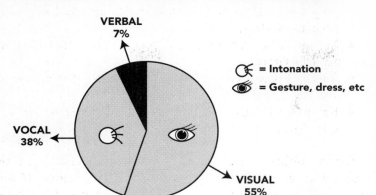

This information is very useful when teaching presentation and public speaking skills. Most people find it hard to believe that the visual aspect of communication has by far the greatest impact. Most think that the verbal aspects of the message—the words you actually say—are the most important. Wrong, as Figure 12 shows. What people *see* does not only include things such as projected slides and documentation for formal presentations, it also includes the way we present ourselves; our facial expressions, body language, our clothes and our grooming. It is naive to underestimate the visual impact we can have on people. We usually refer to the combination of all of these things as a person's *image*.

There are a number of reasons why it is important to pay attention to developing a positive visual image:

- *What people see they believe*—remember, as we have already discussed what people see affects their perception of you.
- *First impressions count*—statistics suggest that within 10 seconds of meeting someone we have already started developing our assumptions about the person. Make sure those first impressions count.

- *Being well dressed and well groomed is part of the total professional package.* It adds perceived value to your competence and confidence.

Dress

A lot of organisations seem to be slowly relaxing their dress requirements. There is a growing realisation that there is little correlation between the way a person dresses and their ability to perform a task. However, it would be safe to say that the ice is thawing extremely slowly and there are still very strong expectations in relation to dress codes in most organisations. These codes, often unspoken, have been around for many years and are well entrenched in our social culture. In some organisations, such as banks and charted accountancy firms, the codes are very strict and formal. In other organisations, like fashion agencies and art studios, the dress codes are very casual. In fact, one organisation I work with has only one real dress code—please wear shoes!

This discussion begs the question 'are the clothes we wear really important?'. It depends on the organisation, and the industry, in which you work. Once again, the way we dress sends a message to the people we are dealing with. Sloppy dress, sloppy mind, sloppy work. Would you trust a person to invest a million dollars of your money if they were wearing a pair of frayed jeans, sandals and dreadlocks? It's all about perception.

When considering how you dress:

- Take a good look around your organisation and determine what the most successful people wear. This obviously applies to both men and women. To the degree that you are comfortable, wear a similar 'level' of clothing. If most people wear 'sloppy casual' and the more successful people wear 'smart casual', with which group would you prefer to be associated?
- Always dress to the level of the organisation to which you aspire.
- Identify someone specific who fills a role to which you aspire and use them as a benchmark for your own dress.

■ Always, without compromise, dress appropriately.

For those wanting to do it properly, seek out an 'image consultant'. This may seem over the top, but these people can provide you with some incredibly valuable advice that will put you ahead of the crowd in the trust and respectability stakes by ensuring you dress appropriately. While it will cost substantially, the advice will be worth every cent.

Individual style

Often people tell me that the way they are 'expected' to dress cramps their personal style. Sure, we should all be more enlightened and insightful and realise that a person's clothing cannot and does not reflect their ability. Unfortunately, dress perceptions are deeply ingrained in our thinking and the *reality* is that most organisations are very conservative. Try to express your personal style within the current codes of dress your organisation has set. Your dress should match the culture of your organisation and if you feel so inhibited by the dress codes that are expected, then maybe you are in the wrong organisation. Simply put, if you can't conform to the dress codes you will be very unlikely to go far in the organisation.

Grooming

Grooming does matter. I knew a person once who earned very good money and bought very expensive suits. The problem was that he wore them like hessian bags and failed to support the costly outfit with some of the finer detail. He could have been wearing the cheapest suit available for all the difference it made. There are any number of books or image consultants that can help you with the definitive detail of grooming.[3] It is sufficient here to say that grooming is an important part of the overall message you send out to

---

3 Some good books on the subject include:
   S. Morem (1997) *How to Gain the Professional Edge*, Better Books, Chicago, Ill; J. T. Molloy (1996) *New Women's Dress for Success*, Warner Books, New York; S. Bixler and N. Nix-Rice (1997) *The New Professional Image*, Adams, Avon, Mass.; and V. Seitz (1997) *Your Executive Image*, Adams, Avon, Mass.

people. Being well dressed and well groomed sends a message that you pay attention to detail, that you are capable and confident.

If you really want to make changes in your grooming, seek some professional input. See an image consultant, or a colour consultant to advise on things like make up, hair colour or style and clothing colours to suit skin tone. Always go to a good hairdresser.

Failure to pay attention to the detail of grooming could cost you dearly in the long run. Take the time to look at yourself critically, and if you're game, seek the input of someone who will give you honest but constructive input regarding your dress and grooming. If you can't do it yourself, and you can't find someone to help, spend the money and find an image consultant that will help. Considering the statistics we discussed earlier and that 55 per cent of the impact you have on others comes from your visual presentation—it *is* worth the effort!

Chapter 4

USING NETWORKS TO CREATE POSITIVE POLITICAL ENVIRONMENTS

NETWORKS, RELATIONSHIPS AND INFLUENCE

'A dwarf on a giant's shoulders sees farther of the two.'

George Herbert

People and relationships are the basis and context for everything we do and, as organisations restructure and redevelop themselves, the importance of networks and valuable professional relationships as the means for oiling the wheels of industry and getting things done is becoming even more significant. Not many people can claim they conduct their work in complete isolation. As John Donne said, 'no man is an island, entire of itself'.

When developing a positive political environment, co-operative relationships between people are the canvas on which the painting is done. If you are to succeed in business or to progress your career you *must* learn the skills required to develop networks of relationships that you can use to influence others and to find the information and resources you need to achieve your goals. Simply put, you just can't do it on your own. If there is only one thing you can focus on to create for yourself a positive environment, focus on the development of positive and influential relationships. Independent of your basic functional competence, there is nothing more significant you can do to advance your personal cause—at the end of the day strong, positive relationships will *always* serve you well.

In today's organisation there is a greater emphasis on the individual's need to achieve specific goals and objectives. There is a tendency for fewer rules and procedures and more room for individual initiative and performance. People are required to move across traditional departmental borders and to work outside previously established channels of authority to gain information and activate resources in order to meet internal and external demands and expectations creatively. This requires great interpersonal dexterity and the ability to manoeuvre your way through the organisational and personal politics that come with the territory. Those who are by nature politically adept do this with style and grace. They develop vast networks and complex interpersonal structures they can tap at any time to find information and resources or to provide the leverage they need to get things done.

In the past, those who have been most successful in organisations have often wielded power and authority like a bludgeon. They succeeded through their effective use of 'hard' skills such as finance and statistics, and were able to 'command and control' staff, usually through threats and fear. Mostly, they employed negative politics to achieve their goals. In current and emerging organisational climates such skills do not hold the advantage they used to. Those who possess the so-called 'soft skills', such as interpersonal effectiveness and communication, are more likely to have greater political influence and consequently achieve greater results. If you are to master the political situations facing you in your organisation you must develop a range of these 'soft skills' and weave for yourself a vast fabric of professional network contacts.

There is no doubt that building relationships and networks of contacts is time consuming and hard work, but the outcomes of your efforts will be more than justified. Some of the benefits will include:

- the ability to exert a greater amount of influence through the help and support of others
- greater personal power through the effective use of your resources

- a higher success rate for the tasks you aim to complete
- the ability to get things done faster and more effectively
- an increased sense of ownership among those with whom you are working
- more job opportunities through a broader contact base
- the opportunity to be promoted faster through more effective work.

What is a professional network?

To build an efficient and effective professional network and reap the enormous benefits there are to be gained takes a great deal of time and effort. For those of you who pride yourselves on your independence and self-reliance it will require a major mental shift as you begin to realise your personal limitations and how much more effective you can be with the help and support of others. Those of you who are 'loners' and not particularly comfortable with people in any shape or form will probably find this task the most difficult. Those of you who enjoy relating to people will find this task the easiest but your challenge will be focusing on developing and maintaining constructive professional relationships that will enhance your political situation and not just make you feel good.

Let's start by examining the nature of networks and the relationships involved. A professional network is

> *a broad range of professional, interpersonal contacts and acquaintances developed over time that enhance and support your career by supplying information and/or resources or exerting influence on your behalf.*

We build professional networks in a very similar way to the way we build our everyday social infrastructures. The socialisation process involves the establishment of shared likes and dislikes, common interests, hobbies and experiences. Think about meeting someone at a dinner party or some other social gathering. All of the initial questions you ask the person you have just met seek to establish common ground.

- 'So, tell me Ted, whereabouts do you live?'
- 'Have you belonged to the club long?'
- 'What do you for a living?'

When we finally uncover some common ground, we use it as a starting point for building the relationship.

'Oh, you play netball at the centre. I played last year but was too busy this season. You would probably know Rachel—she coaches the west city team.'

We seek to establish commonality and then use that as a base on which to build. When building professional relationships in a business context the difference is that the common ground we establish tends to centre on business and professional issues rather than personal interests and shared experiences and preferences. That is not to say that relationships that start off on a professional basis can't evolve into personal friendships as well—many of our closest personal friendships are first established in a professional forum.

There are, however, a number of basic differences between social and professional networks, shown in Table 5.

Table 5 Differences between professional and social networks

Social networks	Professional networks
Built on common personal interests	Built on common professional interests
Usually meet by accident	Meet by design
Seek mutual interests	Professional interests are often previously established
Don't seek personal gain from the relationship	Mutual benefit is the basis of the relationship
Usually based on similar personality styles	Personality style is irrelevant

The nature of network relationships

Unlike most organisational structures no strict hierarchy exists within network relationships. Regardless of a person's position in an organisation or industry, communication in a professional network situation is based on equity and the mutual sharing of ideas, information and resources. Every individual's input has value because it is presented from a context outside your own. The information is taken, synthesised through our own experiences and circumstances, where we precipitate out the things which can add value to our own situation. The best people to network with are usually those who impart information which can improve your personal performance or give you another perspective on your professional initiatives.

> **To get the information and resources you need, use the knowledge and experience of others. This is the great benefit of networking.**

Network relationships are two-way, representing a mutual sharing of ideas, information and resources. They are about co-operation, help, support and providing assistance with the understanding that our efforts will be reciprocated as required.

Yoshii

At the age of 26, Yoshii was extremely young to hold the position of General Manager, Human Resource Development for Sonic Computer Services (SCS). She knew this, and she was also smart enough to know that her promotion into this position was not solely due to her 'exceptional' talent. A combination of her hard work, plus the fact the previous person in the role had left without warning and it was easier for management to promote her into the role than recruit someone else, created the opportunity for her. Yoshi was not complaining—she was more concerned about making the most of this opportunity that had played into her hands.

Yoshii sat cross-legged on her lounge at home. She was wearing her 'domestic grunge', as she termed it, red woollen socks, large sloppy pullover and baggy track pants, a small notebook computer perched on her lap. Josie, her flatmate, walked in and put a glass of red wine in front of her on the coffee table.

'Jose, I need some help here. These are the facts. I have been promoted "slightly", and I emphasise "slightly", beyond my capabilities. But I fully intend to make sure I am up to speed and doing a great job within three months—I reckon I have that long to prove myself or get caught out. Any suggestions how I might accomplish this miracle without the obvious brain transplant?'

Josie, who was also wearing her 'domestic grunge' but had added a 'birdsnest' hairdo, had curled herself up on the chair opposite and proceeded to eat a bowl of cereal— it was dinner time. Between mouthfuls she mumbled, 'Bludge off other people's ideas, that's what I do!'

Yoshii didn't understand. 'What do you mean, bludge off other people's ideas—there is no "other people", I'm it!'

Josie put her bowl down and leant forward shaking her head.

'No, you don't understand what I mean.'

At 27, Josie was only slightly older and more experienced. She had graduated in psychology and was currently doing a supervised year in order to practise as a clinical psychologist.

'I do it all the time. You know I have this supervisor this year, well, apart from debriefing my cases, if I need some input or advice I just give her a call and we talk it through. She has helped me heaps in the last few months.'

'But I don't have a supervisor I can turn to.'

Josie picked up her glass of wine and relaxed back into the chair. 'No,' she agreed, 'but you can find one.'

'How?' Yoshii was intrigued.

'You can find lots actually. One of the other things that has really helped me is keeping in touch with a lot of the people I went to uni with. They are in a similar situation to me, so we get together regularly for coffee or a drink to compare notes and share experiences.'

Yoshii sat opposite, her brow knitted, thinking.

'You could be on to something here. I knew sharing a flat with you could have its benefits. So, how would I go about using these contacts?'

'Easy, let's start by making a list of the people you went to uni with who you know are in similar jobs to you.'

Yoshii's fingers started to fly across the keyboard of her computer.

'There's about eight.'

'Do you have their phone numbers? Contact those ones first. What about people in more senior positions, roles like the one you are about to fill.'

'I don't really know anyone.'

'Come on, think, there must be someone.'

'I met a guy at a workshop about a month ago who is in a 'similarish' sort of role.'

'Great, he'll do. Give him a call tomorrow and arrange to meet.'

'What am I going to say?'

'Just tell him you want some advice. Tell him you are taking on a new role and thought he was the best, don't tell him the only, person to talk to. Make it casual. Meet for coffee or something.'

Yoshii sat in silence looking at her computer screen.

'I've only got three months, what else am I going to do?'

'Well, you need to develop other contacts big time. I suggest you start attending every professional function, workshop, conference and cocktail party known to mankind. I also suggest you wear your best corporate outfit and charm everyone's socks off. Then identify those people who can help you the most, take them to lunch and pick their brains.'

'Sounds like exploitation to me.'

'Professional exploitation, thank you very much. Of course, the other side of the coin is one day they will ask you for help of some kind. It's kind of a bartering system

> for intellectual property—it is actually an extremely important part of doing business these days.'
>
> Yoshii leant over and topped up Josie's wine glass and said in an affected voice, 'So, tell me, do you come here often?'
>
> 'Gee, Yosh, you're going to have to think of a better opening line than that!'

In this situation Yoshii is in desperate need for support and advice. She lacks the necessary experience to be successful in her new role. The best way for her to get the information and resources she needs is to use the knowledge and experience of others. This is one of the greatest benefits of networking.

Internal and external networks

It is important to remember that politically, the casual relationships you develop both internal and external to your organisation, can be even more powerful than the formal structures and systems that exist. The cultivation of a broad range of constructive and mutually beneficial relationships will give you a distinct political edge. Just because you are placed high in the structure of your organisation doesn't necessarily mean you are well connected—in fact, it is very likely that the person who maintains the organisation's desktop computers knows more people and is owed more favours, consequently holding significantly more influence within the organisation.

Internal networks

As organisations continue to flatten and reorganise themselves into vastly different forms, the ability to build comprehensive and effective networks internally is becoming increasingly important. The need to be more responsive to customer needs and more flexible in meeting customer expectations requires the skill to develop internal network relationships.

To achieve personal and organisational objectives you need to work across departmental barriers to gain co-operation and assistance. Your ability to build informal relationships with people in other departments will be crucial.

Internal network relationships can help you by:

- providing information otherwise unavailable or hard to access
- cutting red tape and speeding response and process times
- gaining the support of numbers for your ideas or suggestions
- ensuring co-operation when it is required
- broadening your personal ability to influence
- giving you optional means for getting things done.

Build an effective internal network and you significantly increase your political influence within the organisation and your ability to achieve the things important to you.

External networks

External networks consist of the contacts you develop outside your organisation that assist you to do your job more effectively. Typically, but not always, your external network will include people who are in the same profession or industry who can provide information or assistance on specific topics.

These contacts can come from a range of different areas including:

- previous jobs
- professional organisations
- training workshops
- school, college or university friends
- conferences
- trade shows
- product launches
- informal contacts made at parties, weddings, the kids' sports teams and so on.

103

You can meet people from a similar or the same industry or profession almost anywhere. The common factor is your professional interest, which becomes the basis for continued contact. These relationships must be strategically and purposefully developed—you must make the effort to establish contact and look for ways to maintain the relationship over time. It is also necessary to review and analyse the value a professional relationship is adding to your career, so that you only put time into those professional relationships that add value. (I'm not suggesting, however, that this is a sound approach to take with your personal relationships.)

Juliet

'Paula, it's Juliet. Missed you at the forum last night. Did you have a better offer?'

'Juliet, hi! I did have a better offer actually and I am not telling you about it over an open telephone line, that's for sure.'

Juliet and Paula met at a Law Reform conference sponsored by the government two years ago. They had been together in a workgroup responsible for producing a paper outlining recommended changes with an emphasis on the female perspective. They had spent a great deal of time together at the conference and found that apart from sharing the same profession, they had a lot more in common. Both women, both in the law, both fighting the 'old boys' network that haunted the profession—both very ambitious. Following the conference they had kept in touch and had become a constant source of support to one another.

'Paula, I am working on a case at the moment and can't find any precedent to use in my defence. I thought I remembered you talking about . . .'

Juliet had remembered correctly, however it wasn't Paula but one of her colleges who had the information.

'Look, I'll give Robert a call and let him know you are going to ring him. He is a bit hard to catch at times, but he will be only too happy to help. He's a good person to know. In fact, I should get you together for a coffee.'

Paula put them in touch and Juliet got the valuable information she required to win the case.

External networks expand your sphere of influence and give you the opportunity to improve your abilities. They broaden your resource base, provide you with a greater range of ideas and give you more options and possibilities. They also allow you to access information much faster and use the knowledge and experience of others as if it was your own.

The network web

To try to simplify the notion of network relationships, think of a spider's web where you form the central point. Within this web there are three main areas.

1. *Influence network*—these are the contacts you have, both internal and external to your organisation, that can exert the most influence.
2. *Information network*—these contacts are not as valuable as those in your Influence network, but they are still able to provide information and/or resources and to put you in contact with other people who can give assistance.
3. *Expert network*—this is the network of people you form based on your association with profession-specific groups.

Figure 13 shows how these networks operate together. Let's have a look at each of them in a little more detail.

Influence networks

The relationships you develop in your *Influence network* have the greatest impact on the creation of your positive political

Figure 13 The network web

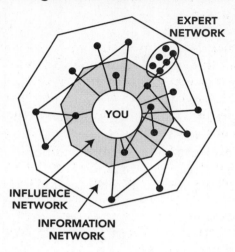

environment. They provide you with the most relevant information and/or the most useful resources. They can pull the best 'strings' in the shortest possible time and give you the most relevant and useful advice. By virtue of their value, these are the relationships on which you should spend most of your time and effort—they are the closest to you on the web. These people are equipped to provide you with the help and support you need to succeed and, what's more, for a wide range of reasons, they are interested in you succeeding. Mentors, guides, sponsors or role models form part of the Influence network and are perhaps the relationships that provide us with the most significant input.

People in your Influence network:

- work in the same or similar profession or industry
- are well positioned, often in a more senior or influential role
- have more, better or different knowledge and experience
- have access to a broad range of information and resources
- are recognised by your profession or industry as leaders in their field
- chair industry or professional bodies

- have an excellent network of their own contacts that you can utilise.

If you are lucky, people with these qualities will 'wander' into your work life and relationships will develop naturally. However, experience suggests that these types of relationships are reasonably hard to come by and often need to be sourced and strategically developed. This may seem rather cold and calculating when compared to personal relationships but remember, professional relationships commence with the understanding that you are seeking mutual benefit. You don't necessarily have to like the person, although there is a lot more to be gained if you can factor in friendship as a component of the relationship.

When considering possible candidates for your Influence network, ask yourself questions such as:

- Where are the gaps in my skills and knowledge?
- What types of resources and information do I need?
- What types of contacts do I need?
- What associations will improve my ability to influence?
- Who do I know who has insight into the personalities, structure and politics of my organisation?
- Who is recognised by my profession as a leader in their field?

Spend the majority of your networking time on the development and maintenance of your Influence network, as it has the capacity to produce the best returns—political influence, personal achievement and career progression. Under normal circumstances you might only develop between five and 10 Influence relationships at any given time. These are not necessarily lifetime relationships either, as it is likely there will come a time when you will 'outgrow' the relationship and need to seek input at a higher level. There are no set rules to how these relationships work—it is very much dependent on the personalities of the individuals involved and the nature of the situation surrounding those individuals.

Information networks

The predominant role of the *Information network* is to provide you with a far broader base of information and resources. As shown in Figure 13, it lies further from you and by nature requires less time to maintain. The people who form this part of your professional network are often referred to as 'contacts' and 'acquaintances', people you talk to perhaps once every three or four months just to keep in touch or more often when you are asking them for information and resources.

Consequently, it is wise to have as many people in your Information network as you can handle, since it is reasonably inexpensive timewise. Often you meet these people through industry functions or professional conferences, establish your professional common ground, develop a certain rapport and keep in touch, sharing ideas and staying abreast of each others' work initiatives. Call them when you are faced with a situation that is unfamiliar to you or when you need experienced input on a specific topic.

People in your Information network:

- work in the same industry or profession
- hold a position very similar to your own
- are at a similar level within their organisation
- face similar problems and complexities in their work
- have a wider or different information and resource base
- are open and willing to share
- see value in the information and resources you can offer them.

As with all network contacts, you need to seek to develop your Information network strategically. Actively seek out people who can extend your information and resources, establish a professional acquaintance and keep in touch. These types of relationships are usually easier to develop and maintain than those in your Influence network—they require less time and effort and contribute at a lower level of impact.

When considering the development of your Information network, ask yourself questions such as:

- Where can I best meet people in similar roles to mine?
- What information and resources would best benefit me?
- Is this person fulfilling similar tasks to myself?
- Is their organisation of similar size and operation as my own?
- Are they facing similar problems?
- Will I extend my information and resource base through this relationship?

Information networks are fluid by nature. While some people will remain part of this network for years, most will come and go depending upon the value individuals can contribute at any time. To maintain an effective Information network:

- *Keep regular contact*—it is a good idea to keep a list and record who you contact when.
- *Regularly review your list*—make sure you are using your time wisely and the relationships you have formed add value to your situation.
- *Top it up*—always be on the lookout for people who can become a part of your network.

Expert networks

Expert networks actually form part of your Information network, but they focus more closely on the technical or specific interest areas of your work. Typically they consist of those people you meet through the professional bodies that represent your industry or profession. It is possible for contacts in the Expert network to be part of your Influence or Information networks. This network is particularly useful for gaining specific expert knowledge and information.

In Influence and Information networks *you* form the hub of the network and take responsibility for its function and maintenance. Generally, in an Expert network you are not the hub but merely part of the overall web.

The Expert network centres around professional or special interests designed to give you the expert knowledge to be more effective at your job. Use your Expert networks to extend your Information network—the people you meet this way can provide broader and ongoing information and resources.

Expert networks can include:

- special interest groups within professional organisations
- industry task forces
- self-development groups such as Dale Carnegie or Toastmasters
- specialised Internet bulletin boards, list servers and chat rooms.

Relationships formed in the Expert network provide you with specific detail about specific issues relevant to your success.

Ned

'Ned, I think this is a wonderful idea,' the GM put Ned's proposal on the table and took off his glasses, 'but . . .'. Ned braced himself for the bad news he knew always followed the word 'but'.

'. . . But it will require capital outlay that has not been allowed for in this year's budget.'

Ned's proposal suggested establishing a new technical sales division to capitalise on an unprecedented interest in recent technologies. The benefits to the organisation and possible revenue generation would be substantial, but first there was this hurdle to get over.

'Considering the opportunity to capture this market earlier than our competitors and the distinctly realistic revenue possibilities, wouldn't it be in our best interest to find an alternative way around the budget problem?'

Ned thought he should at least try to explore some options.

'I can't disagree with that, Ned. I commend you on your ability to identify this opportunity and develop a way of capitalising on it.'

There was a pause—a long pause.

'Ned, let me throw you a challenge and, believe me, I see it as a fairly significant challenge. If you can come up with a proposal that sees the financing of this project come from someone's—I don't care whose—budget, then we will do it. You know how tightly everyone hangs on to their budget dollars, so I'm not sure that you will be able to generate any interest. However, I wish you luck. I really do hope you can make this work.'

As he walked back to his office, Ned thought 'Excellent! The really hard thing is going to be making this seem like it was difficult.' Ned was well liked in the organisation and being head of Technical Resource Management had given him the opportunity to build a wide range of very useful relationships. Ned had said quite openly on a number of occasions, 'At some stage every manager is going to have to ask me a favour—which suits me fine.' His theory was that everyone developed 'favour collateral' that could be drawn upon at any given time. You have to grant favours to get favours, so Ned was always willing to help people in any way he could, knowing that one day he would need help in return.

By the time he got back to his office he had clearly identified the three key people he needed to get on side, and more importantly, the three people whose budgets he wanted to raid.

Sitting down at his desk Ned picked up the telephone and dialled Leone Summers, Director of Imaging.

'Leone, Ned here. What's on for lunch? One p.m.'s great—see you at Bell's Café.' Leone had been a friend and cohort for many years. On more than one occasion they had collaborated on initiatives that were of mutual benefit. Ned knew Leone was having a problem penetrating certain aspects of her market—maybe they could kill two birds with one stone.

He immediately dialled again. He got the voicemail of Reg Gardener, Director of Information Technology Outsourcing.

'Hey Reg, it's me, Ned. You still on for golf on Sunday?

I told Margy I'd be home about five p.m. That should give us time for a couple of drinks at the nineteenth hole. Give me a yell if you have a problem with that. There is one work issue we will need to discuss on Sunday—only one, I promise. See ya then.'

Ned and Reg had been friends for a number of years. Their friendship had started early in their careers, when they had both attended a conference on the legal implications of intellectual property. It was so boring that on the second afternoon Reg had suggested their time could be better utilised on the golf course. They had been firm friends ever since. While Ned did not want to exploit their long-time friendship, he did know that Reg kept a 'slush fund' for 'unexpected opportunities'. Ned had an unexpected opportunity.

Ned hung up from Reg and paused as he thought about the next call. Maria Theopoulos, Director of Marketing, while certainly not an adversary, was not as close a relationship as Reg or Leone. He dialled.

'Maria, glad I caught you. Ned here from TRM. How's it going?' There was a small amount of social chatter.

'Maria, I have some good news for you, I have been able to convince the GM to allocate your two graduates to my trainee resource budget.' Maria was extremely pleased and thanked Ned for pushing things through for her, since this allowed her to employ two more graduates to bolster her under-resourced team.

'Maria, will you be around on Tuesday afternoon? I just need to talk to you about a project the GM has thrown in my lap. I think you may be able to help me.' They made the appointment. Maria was only too happy to help.

'How long has it been, Ned, since we last spoke?' The GM looked at Ned over the top of his glasses.

'About a week and a half, I think.'

'Hmm—I'd like to know how you got Maria on side so quickly.' Ned just smiled. 'Well, OK—let's do it!'

Over the years, Ned had developed associations and friendships that allowed him to create a win/win/win situation easily. By calling on his network and working co-operatively with the significant players in this scenario, Ned was able to achieve his objective. Would Ned have been able to achieve the same result if he had not spent the time developing these network relationships? Perhaps—but certainly not as swiftly or with the same ease.

Establishing professional relationships

An old Jewish proverb suggests that 'those who want friends must first show themselves friendly'. It is not realistic in a networking environment to expect people to come up to you and establish contact. It is *your* responsibility—be pro-active and go out of your way to talk to people and be friendly. Many people find it extremely difficult to walk into a room full of strangers and start making small conversation. Unfortunately, this is one of the major methods for developing network contacts and you will need to refine your skills in this area if you are going to develop an effective professional network.

Pressing the flesh

Here are some tips to help make the daunting task of initial contact easier:

- *Just do it.* Rather than thinking too long and hard about what you are going to say, jump straight in and start talking.
- *Develop a set of opening statement and running questions.* 'Hi! My name is Mark, nice to meet you.' The laws of reciprocity suggest that the person will respond by giving their name. Questions you can ask include: Where do you work? What sort of work do you do? What qualifications do you have? Where did you study? What area do you specialise in? Are you a member of the professional association?
- *Ask people questions about themselves.* The most boring person you will ever talk to is the one who can only tell you about themselves.

113

- *Listen actively.* Show interest with your responses and body language, concentrate on what the person is saying and ask questions that relate to the topic.
- *Seek common ground.* People feel more comfortable when they can identify areas of commonality. Seek these out and establish them firmly. This builds rapport and develops association.
- *Have an opinion.* Don't be too opinionated, but don't avoid asserting your opinion. Listen to and respect the opinions of others.
- *Find a way to help.* If you have identified a person as a valuable network contact, in the course of your conversation seek to uncover areas where they need assistance and you can help. Offer to send a copy of an article, the name of a book or the phone number of a person to contact. This provides the basis for developing ongoing contact.
- *Always be prepared.* Remember that this is an exercise in self-promotion. Make sure you take business cards. A pen and small pad is useful in case you need to send information or take down other details.
- *Keep moving.* It is easy to get 'stuck' with one or two people at a function. Easy because you can rapidly find a comfort zone and avoid having to break the ice with someone new. Set yourself a goal of a specific number of new people you intend to meet during the function and keep moving.
- *Follow through.* Make sure you do the things you said you would do. If you think a person will be a good ongoing contact, get in touch within a week. Make a phone call, arrange coffee—don't let the contact go cold.

Building and maintaining network relationships

Once you have made the initial contact and have determined that there is value in establishing a professional relationship, you must be proactive about building and maintaining it. You are building *relational capital*—by offering value to the relationship, the other person involved will seek to do the same in order to retain balance. When a relationship becomes obviously 'one sided', it is time to move on.

The following aspects of the relationship will grow and mature with time:

- common professional interests
- common personal interests
- mutual respect
- desire to help
- need for help.

There are a range of techniques you can employ to help relationships mature rapidly:

- *Keep in touch*—this is what networking is all about. You don't have any sort of relationship if you are not communicating. You should be in contact with the people who form your Influence network every two to three weeks, if not more often. These people are providing you with valuable insight, information and advice to help you exert political influence and advance your career. Your Information and Expert networks require less regular contact—however it still needs to be regular even if it is every few months. Use the phone, send an email, jot them a note—just keep in touch because when you need them to help you it is handy if they remember who you are.
- *Meet face to face*—it is extremely important to meet face to face with your network contacts occasionally. With your Influence network contacts meetings should be quite regular—once a month. With your Information and Expert networks it can be less often—once every six months. Whether it be for drinks, coffee, breakfast, lunch or dinner or simply calling into their office when you are in the area, it is crucial to meet face to face when you can.
- *Send an article*—as you read your professional journals, business magazines and newspapers look for articles you

think will interest individuals in your network. This will send a number of important messages—they are in your thoughts, you know what they are interested in, you are making a concerted effort to help them. This builds relational capital you can draw upon in the future.

- *Special events*—when you have the ability, invite people on your network to special events that may be of interest to them or will give them an opportunity to meet interesting and valuable people.
- *Do favours*—this is one of the most powerful tools you can use to develop professional relationships. By doing things for people you are once again building relational capital. Refer them for a job, send them a copy of a book, save them a good seat at the seminar, let them use your ideas and materials . . . do lots and lots of favours.
- *Broaden the net*—where possible, introduce people in your network to others who might be able to help them.
- *Respond rapidly*—if you are asked to help, do it quickly and efficiently and don't make it seem like it's a chore.
- *Congratulate*—if a person has been promoted or has achieved a significant success be open and generous with your praise and congratulations. Let them know that you are genuinely pleased for them.

> **Doing things for people is building relational capital. Refer them for a job, save them a good seat at the seminar . . . do lots and lots of favours.**

How you manage and develop your professional networks depends very much on the type of person you are and how you prefer to manage your relationships. There are a number of important points to emphasise:

- *Analyse your current network*—take the time to draw yourself a network map and determine whether your current network is sufficient. Articulate the areas of your network you would like to improve and grow.
- *Establish network goals*—based on the previous information, set yourself network goals and time frames for achievement.
- *Set up systems*—develop a system for recording information on all of your network contacts and a method for maintaining regular contact with each.

Without a sophisticated network of personal and professional relationships, you will be destined to remain a political weakling. Take the time, make the effort and ensure there are large numbers of people both inside and outside the organisation working with you and for you to create a positive political environment.

Chapter 5

HUMAN BEHAVIOUR AND POLITICAL RELATIONSHIPS

UNDERSTANDING HUMAN BEHAVIOUR IN THE WORKPLACE

So we, being many, are one body . . . and every
one members one of another. Having then
gifts differing . . .

Romans 12:4–8

My partner and I call it 'public theatre'; it is one of our favourite pastimes. When we have time to kill, we find the busiest public place possible with ready access to a cappuccino machine and sit for hours watching people act out their lives on the public stage. We try to determine the situations of strangers—married, divorced, first date, mother and daughter, workmates, brothers . . . Who knows if we are right, or even close, but it doesn't really matter because it provides us with endless hours of free entertainment. We are self-confessed 'people-watching junkies'—some would say voyeurs and, we admit, it's true. For us, it is part of our disposition. We love people and love to watch them in action.

When it comes to positioning yourself politically within an organisation 'people watching' skills are incredibly valuable. People who are highly skilled in developing positive political environments have a finely honed talent for observing human behaviour. Through their observations they are able to determine how to respond to the needs of others and how to influence behaviour in order to achieve a win/ win/win situation. They can modify their behaviour on an individual level in order to build rapport. They make people feel comfortable and relaxed in their presence regardless of who they are or what their job or background. For some, such talents of observation are innate—they naturally enjoy interacting with people, observing their behaviour and using the information they gather to achieve mutual goals. Others, however, have very little or no natural talent in this area. Like the computer technician who, while phoning to divert his pager, was heard to mutter, 'Damn, it's a real person. I prefer to deal with machines, they're far more intelligent!' If this is you, then you are starting from ground zero. There is hope, but you are going to have to work really hard.

People are the basic unit, the atom, of all organisational structure and consequently, the basic building block for creating positive political environments. If you have a crystal clear understanding of human behaviour you will behave wisely yourself when it comes to interacting with others to achieve common goals. This chapter very briefly explores human behaviour in the workplace and considers a model to enhance your understanding of people. The objective is to give you a small taste of the subject and, hopefully, to encourage you to explore further this incredibly interesting topic. Become a true student of human behaviour and you will reap the benefits of the valuable insights you gain.

If you become a student of human behaviour you will:

- know what behaviours to use in which situation to gain political advantage
- gain a better insight into your own behaviour, helping you adapt easily to that of others
- have a greater influence over other people's decisions
- find it easier to gather support for your ideas and projects
- easily determine the professional strengths and weaknesses of others
- improve your relationships, particularly with those with whom you have previously been in conflict.

Some extremely good reasons to read on! 119

People are different

People are different. As simple and as obvious as this statement is, the ramifications it should have on our behaviour and how we choose to deal with others often fail to sink in. As individuals we are the centre of our own universe and as much as we try to view situations from the perspective of others our natural disposition is to focus on personal needs. Consequently human interaction is often fraught with conflict and confrontation based on the notion that 'I'm right, you're wrong'. This is obviously not always true. Often there in no 'right' or 'wrong'—just 'different'.

In our study of human behaviour the starting premise is—*it is OK for people to be different*. Once you really believe this notion you will start your journey toward understanding human behaviour. Until then, your observations will lack dimension, they will be lopsided and biased—a flat, black and white image. Your perspective would be a bit like that of the old man who had lived all of his life in a small town in country New Zealand. When asked if he had ever had the desire to travel and see other parts of the world, his response was 'I have read many books about many different parts of the world, I don't really need to go, do I?'. This man's perspective was one-dimensional; he lacked the ability to see the value in gaining firsthand knowledge.

Understanding human behaviour is all about empathy, acceptance and tolerance—seeing good in others and identifying the opportunity to develop synergies for mutual benefit. It is about exploring differences and learning how to work in harmony. People who lack this ability are often arrogant, narrow and insular, expecting everyone to behave like them—and what a boring world that would be.

Bernard and Zu

Bernard entered the private room of the restaurant tentatively. The lights were dimmed, the music loud and lights were flashing wildly. He was dressed in a suit and tie, because that was what he always wore to special occasions and his niece Lianne's eighteenth birthday was a very special occasion.

At 42, Bernard was pleased with his career progress. He was the chief actuary for a small insurance company, with the promise of advancement to bigger opportunities and organisations either in this country or overseas. Ever since he was a child he had loved logic and order and anything to do with numbers or statistics. He had excelled at maths, winning a national competition at 11 and scoring in the top .5 per cent in the country in his final year of school. He spent seven years at university studying his craft before getting his first job. While he was exceedingly comfortable when faced with a mathematical or statistical challenge, or sitting in front of his computer, he was not particularly good with people or in social situations—such as his niece's birthday. He knew he was conservative, very conservative, in most areas of his life but that was his way and he had grown more comfortable with it as he had got older.

Bernard edged into the room and hovered on its dimly-lit edges until he spotted his older brother and his wife sitting with a group of friends and relatives he recognised. He quickly made his way to the group and that is where he stayed the rest of the night, until taking his leave at 10 to prepare for work the next day—Sunday.

Zu burst through the door late at about 9.30, a ball of colour and kinetic energy. At first glance he looked like he was dressed to attend a fancy dress party as a gipsy, but those who knew Zu recognised his normal dress. As soon as he hit the room he was dancing, making his way through the tables, greeting with great gusto everyone he saw, whether he knew them or not. When he reached Lianne sitting on the other side of the room he swept her to her feet and onto the dance floor in one smooth motion, and he threw himself about in crazed delight for the next hour without taking a breath.

Zu was also Lianne's uncle, on her mother's side. At

38, he was the senior creative director for one of the country's largest advertising agencies. He had never been conventional as a child—the world always seemed to move too slowly for Zu, and at 16 he got bored with school and took off to travel the world in search of fame and fortune. For the next six years the family received hastily scribbled postcards or dirty scraps of paper stuffed into equally dirty envelopes from all over the world, telling brief but exciting tales of his adventures. Eventually, he arrived in London and through a friend he had met in a monastery in Tibet secured a job as a buyer in a small advertising agency. Finally Zu had found an outlet for his energy and creativity, one that actually earned him some money.

Zu stayed at Lianne's party until most people had left, then, because it was Lianne's first night as a legal adult, he took her and a few of her friends to a couple of his favourite night clubs. Lianne arrived home at 10 the next morning exhausted. Zu was last seen heading for a new 'day club' he had just discovered.

When you consider Bernard and Zu you could probably not find two completely opposite personalities. Which one is wrong and which is right? Those who are more conservative or introverted will no doubt relate better to Bernard—he seems more stable and reliable—closer to their personality. Those same people may think Zu would be better off in a zoo or living in another universe. Others would much rather spend a night on the town with Zu than with Bernard (me included)—better to be partied to death than bored to death. Still, I defy anyone to establish right or wrong with either of these two people. This is not about right or wrong, but about *difference* and preferred behaviour.

Why do people behave the way they do?

What motivates people to behave the way they do? Answering this age-old question has produced theories ranging from astrology (still a popular belief today) to Aristotle, who suggested that behaviour is the result of the concentration of various fluids in the body, to behaviouralists, who argue that behaviour is set of responses to the stimulus of the environment. Such philosophical questioning spawned the 'science' of psychology that, while generating a great knowledge of the workings of human behaviour, still seeks definitive reasons for why we do the things we do.

Inherited and learned behaviours

The basic foundation for our behaviour is the things we have 'inherited and learned'. This process starts even before we are born and predominantly relates to characteristics we inherit from our parents and immediate family. Values, morals, etiquette and principles start to become part of our psyche from a very young age, significantly influencing our world view. For example, people who are very narrowminded, holding strong, even dogmatic views, are most often reflecting the behaviours of parents, close relatives or siblings with similar behaviour patterns.

During adolescence we often come into conflict with and challenge those things inherited and learned. Eventually we forge our own set of attitudes, beliefs and values as we move into adulthood. Things inherited and learned at a young age still strongly influence our 'attitudes, beliefs and values', but as we grow and start associating in a broader social and work context we begin to develop a more rounded, personalised worldview.

Attitudes, beliefs and values

Our attitudes, beliefs and values are influenced by a wide range of other stimuli as we continue to mature and become distanced from the influence of our immediate family. Influences such as our peers, teachers, the media, childhood heroes, religion, extended family, friends, fashion, trends . . .

Attitudes include such things as our opinions of the opposite sex, social issues, politics, or anything upon which we choose to establish a view.

123

Beliefs are those basic principles by which we live our life, such as the basic right of the individual to live their life as they please, tolerance, acceptance or the existence of God.

Our *values* are the things we consider to be important in our lives and their order of priority—family, work, career, leisure and sport, and so on.

These three areas overlap to form the core of our being— who we really are. Ultimately it is our attitudes, beliefs and values that determine what motivates us to behave the way we do.

Motivation is the trigger for behaviour. We develop certain attitudes, beliefs and values, therefore we behave in certain ways. A person who has attitudes, beliefs and values systems that state that it is extremely important to eat correctly and exercise regularly are consequently motivated to watch their intake of fatty foods and exercise three or four times a week. Another person may a system of attitudes, beliefs and values that dictates that life is about pleasure and indulgence—'live it to the full for however long you have'. They may consequently be motivated to smoke and drink heavily, pay no regard to what they eat—and exercise? Forget it!

Figure 14 The behavioural iceberg

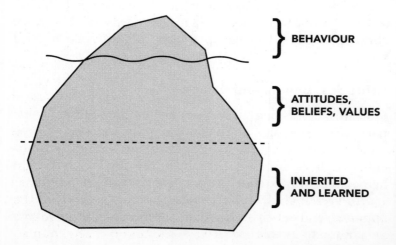

The 'iceberg' illustration in Figure 14 provides a simple model for understanding some of the factors that lie behind human behaviour. Behaviour being exhibited by an individual at any given time is only ever the tip of the iceberg. There are many reasons why people act the way they do, and their behaviour is only the final, and relatively small, end product of an extremely complex and convoluted series of processes. The way we see a person behave is the response to years of character formation, originating from a myriad different sources.

Here is a picture to help illustrate the iceberg theory. A girl of about 18 had been raised in a family where she was abused both psychologically and sexually by her father. What she inherited and learned from this situation was that she had no self-worth and she was only good for the 'pleasures' she provided. She believed that the only way to gain acceptance and affection from the opposite sex was by using her sexuality. The messages she received became a part of her system of beliefs, attitudes and values and consequently motivated her to behave in certain ways. She formed relationships that were destructive with men who were abusive, because she believed this was the way she should be treated. If a man was kind to her, showing her genuine affection and kindness, she would immediately end the relationship. She exhibited severe attention-seeking behaviour, regularly taking drug overdoses and attempting to commit suicide to gain the attention of at least somebody. She did not believe she had any intrinsic worth. Her body language reflected her beliefs—she would never make eye contact, constantly looked to the ground and would avoid conversation and social interaction where possible. Her counsellor's challenge was to help her view herself differently, change her attitudes, beliefs and values about herself and by doing this motivate herself to behave in a way that reflected a more positive self-esteem.

In this chapter, we look only at human *behaviour*—the tip of the iceberg. We do not endeavour to explore the other complex aspects of the human psyche that form or make up our attitudes, beliefs and values. A loose set of guidelines or a framework for observing and interpreting human

125

behaviour in context is developed. This is the starting point for developing a better understanding of people and ways to modify our own behaviour in order to establish greater rapport and more effective interaction.

First impressions count

Have you ever been guilty of meeting a person for the first time, making a snap judgement that you don't like them—only to find after spending a bit more time with them that they are really OK? In a lot of cases, this is the starting point for many successful long-term relationships.

Statistics suggest that we tend to develop reasonably concrete perceptions of others within a few seconds of meeting them, perceptions obviously based on minimal and scatty information. Intuitively, we screen their behaviour, appearance, dress and other visual factors through the filters of our own attitudes, beliefs, and value system, and then formulate our opinions based on our past experience or our own categorisations. Often, we see only what we want to see or what we expect—often we are wrong. One manager, before interviewing someone for a job, would walk through the foyer and look at the candidate before the interview started. He believed that he could tell from that brief observation whether the person would fit and if they were right for the job—his first impression determined how long the interview would take.

Many years ago, on arriving at a conference for counsellors and social workers, I noticed a man registering who was dressed in biker leathers, had long straggly hair with a matching beard and a gallery of tattoos on every visible piece of skin. My personal prejudices told me this man must be part of some obscure department of the public service, that he was uneducated, uncouth and probably bit the heads off chickens for fun. I decided to avoid contact, for fear of contamination. As fate would have it, when the conference first broke into smaller discussion groups he and I were assigned the same topic, which meant we had to work together on a presentation to the conference. I was apprehensive—to say the least. For the first 20 minutes we sat and talked, finding out about each other and why we were attending this conference. To my great surprise, I discovered that this alarming-looking man was a senior minister of a prominent Christian organisation, dedicated to caring for bikers and street kids. I found him to be one of the most gentle, intelligent and caring individuals I had (and have) ever met. We became firm friends and my conservative (and incredibly naive) social views were turned on their ear.

Selective perception creates rigid mindsets that act as barriers to the truth. We tend to reject or react strongly to things that do not fit our personal perceptions. By filtering information through our casual perceptions we interpret it in a way that is comfortable to us— but this approach lacks depth and fails to consider other possibilities. It is safe to say of most people that they are 'more than meets the eye'.

> ## Selective perception creates rigid mindsets that act as barriers to the truth.

If we observe the behaviour of others in an intuitive and unstructured way it can lead us to see only what we want to see. The next section offers a model or a structure for understanding behaviour that will allow you to view people with some depth, using an understanding of your own behaviour as the benchmark. This model will provide you with:

- a simple yet objective way of looking at behaviour
- a method that captures a range of well studied and widely accepted ideas on behaviour
- the ability to see information about people that would not otherwise been apparent.

Predicting how your colleagues will react

How an individual acts or reacts in any given situation depends upon personal preference. When faced with a new task or idea some people will predictably step back and consider it thoroughly, others will, just as predictably, roll up their sleeves and jump in feet first. Some will consider the social implications and the impact it may have on the people involved, others will start by asking hard questions about the financial viability of the venture. How we act and react is a result of our attitudes, beliefs and values formed since childhood. The more certain behaviours received positive reinforcement, the more we emulated that behaviour—until we each developed for ourselves a set of behavioural patterns that we follow in given situations. The more we repeat these patterns, the more they are reinforced, the more they make us feel comfortable, the more we continue to repeat them. By the time we reach maturity we all have fairly established behavioural patterns. Many of these behavioural patterns are so much a part of us that we are blind to their very existence.

We consistently use our own behavioural norms as a means of judging the behaviour of others. How many times have you said that so and so is 'strange'? By whose standards? Your own, of course! By becoming aware of our own behaviour patterns we can give ourselves the ability and opportunity to understand and reshape our behaviour in relation to others.

The study of human behaviour assumes that these patterns are predictable under normal circumstances and, this being the case, it is possible to develop a model to determine and interpret human behaviour.

Roslyn and Michael

'You have reached the voicemail of Michael Worth in Occupational Health and Safety. If you wish to leave a message, please do so after the tone, or press zero to be connected to an operator now. Thanks for your call.'

'Michael, this is Roslyn McGuire. I need to see you in my office quick smart. Give me a call.'

Roslyn McGuire was the production manager of a medium sized cosmetics manufacturer. She had been with the organisation since its days as a fledgling player in the industry and risen through the ranks as the company grew through increased consumer interest in natural cosmetics and greater environmental awareness. She had started as a production worker packing boxes and filling distributor orders. Through sheer hard work and a singular focus on getting the job done she was promoted to a supervisor's position and then started to move up through the management ranks. After nearly 10 years of dedication and commitment she was appointed to production manager—an achievement of which she was very proud. If asked to sum up the principles of her success, Roslyn would reply, 'Be tough, then get tougher'.

She believed in keeping her staff on their toes: 'Don't let them get complacent, always keep them guessing'. Her call to Michael Worth was, to use her words, 'to put a bomb under him'. She did not think the OHS committee was addressing the main issues fast enough. She knew that if she was in control of things, a lot more would have been done by now.

Michael, on the other hand, was very different. He had spent the earlier part of his career working as a aged care and guidance counsellor for the social services department. He had decided to move into corporate life and felt that his current skills would be best transferred to a role in the OHS area. He was an extremely pleasant and caring man who engendered an enormous amount of respect among his fellow workers. He was no dynamo, but he did his job well and people trusted him. Michael's philosophy of life was 'There is good in everyone—in some it's just harder to find'. He believed in the intrinsic goodness of human kind and sought to establish harmony and consensus, avoiding conflict wherever possible. This approach was causing delays to certain decisions that had to be made by the OHS committee.

When Michael retrieved his voicemail and heard Roslyn's message, he felt sick in the pit of his stomach. He knew this was not going to be a pleasant experience and he had no doubt who was going to be the casualty.

'You know what your problem is, Michael? You're not tough enough.' Michael sat quietly in front of Roslyn's desk, not game to say a word.

'You need to push these people a lot harder. This is a holiday for them. When they are in these OHS meetings, they're not working, are they? Of course they want them to drag out—they'll let them go on all summer, if you allow it. I bet they want to start having the meetings outside on the grass, don't they?'

Michael had nothing to say. He knew that all she wanted him to do was listen.

'Now I want you to go and organise the next meeting. Kick some butt and get some decisions, do you understand?'

'Yes, Roslyn, I certainly do.'

'Good, that's more like it. OK. Talk to you soon. Right?'

Michael left Roslyn's office predictably depressed. This wasn't the first time he had sat through a meeting like that with her. In fact, they had been happening more regularly over the last month.

He walked into his office, collapsed into his chair and sat staring at the wall. It was clear to Michael that Roslyn basically wanted him to behave like her, adopt her management style and philosophies. He knew he could never do that.

He picked up his pen and started writing his letter of resignation.

Roslyn and Michael are two very different people looking at their work from extremely diverse perspectives. Michael is politically disadvantaged in this situation because Roslyn has far more position power than he does in the structure of the organisation. She can 'pull rank' on him and make him do what she wants, which in this case she is endeavouring to do. However, Roslyn needs to ask herself if this is in fact the best strategy to ensure a win/win/win situation. If Michael goes ahead and resigns then she loses his skills, knowledge and experience, and incurs the costs and delays of looking for a replacement. There is no doubt that Michael needs to be more assertive and to push for greater results from the OHS committee but, equally, Roslyn needs to help him achieve this objective rather than impose her own style and try to make him behave as she would.

As objective observers it is easy for us to see where the difficulties lie and had how personal behavioural differences have caused a significant conflict in this situation. But how can people like Roslyn and Michael, who are in the middle of situations like this, see their differences for themselves and behave in such a way that there is an all-round win? If they both had an understanding of each other's behavioural style it would have been far easier for each of them to know how to respond. Roslyn would have realised the futility of trying to make Michael behave in a way that is way outside of his comfort zone or personality and adapted other strategies to more successfully communicate what she wanted to achieve. Michael would have realised the truth in what Roslyn was trying to say and the problems he has in this area. He could have sought to benefit from her experience and gained some advice on how to adapt his behaviour to get better results from the committee.

A person experienced in observing human behaviour would spot the patterns in the Roslyn/Michael interplay immediately. Roslyn's response to Michael's perceived procrastination was predictable; Michael's response to Roslyn's hard-nosed efforts to rectify the situation were also predictable—by understanding the behavioural styles model these patterns will become clear.

Behavioural Styles Model

The study of human behaviour must start with a better understanding of yourself. In fact, the better you understand your own behaviour and the way you react and interact in a range of varying circumstances, the better you will be equipped to manage the way you deal with others. Your objective must not be to determine how you can 'change others'—that is an impossibility—your objective must be to establish how you can adapt *your* behaviour to generate the preferred behaviour from others or to elicit the most favourable response. By gaining a better understanding of yourself, you will gain more insight into the behaviour of others.

The Behavioural Styles Model (BSM) is only a model. Models are not definitive by nature, neither are they applicable in every situation. Models are based on generalisations and provide a frame of reference by which to make assessments under normal circumstances. There are always exceptions to the rule—there will always be people you know who don't quite fit any of the styles defined by the model. However, having trained literally thousands of people to understand and apply the principles contained in this chapter, I know that there is truth and value to be gained through the application of the BSM.

In learning about the BSM, however, let me suggest you remain cautious of the following:

- *Don't put people in boxes.* Although this model will define behavioural categories and encourage you to align yourself and others within these, be careful not to lock people into these categories too rigidly. Think of the styles more as four poles in the ground and a person's behaviour as being closer to one of the poles than the others.
- *Use the styles only as an indicator.* Don't fall into the temptation of 'labelling' people by a style and referring to them by that name when they behave typically. Apart from being annoying, it narrows your perceptions of the individual and will leave you unprepared if they produce behaviours you weren't expecting.
- *Remember, everyone has all of the styles.* Each person will, to some degree, exhibit qualities of all of the four styles

outlined. Usually they will be more dominant in one of the styles than the others, however, all of the styles are present to some degree.

- Behaviour is only one aspect of the human psyche. As we have already seen, the human psyche is multifaceted and although current behaviour is a valuable and quite reliable indicator of future behaviour, there are other factors that come into play and affect an individual's behaviour.

Carl Jung first published the English translation of his research on human behaviour in his book *Psychological Types*, in 1923. He challenged Freud's notion that the basic human drive was *eros* (sex drive or libido), suggesting rather that all human beings have 'preferences' for certain 'functions' and that preference for a given function is a characteristic, allowing us therefore to be 'typed' or 'classified' by our preferences. Jung suggested that these 'preferences' fell into four main categories: sensing, feeling, thinking and intuition. Since then there have been many models designed to transfer this information into practical, useable tools. One of the most popular—the Myers Briggs Type Indicator (MBTI)—was developed by the mother and daughter team of Katharine Briggs and Isabel Myers, and tested extensively in the 1950s and 1960s. Other models, such as DiSC and Wilson Learning Social Styles, are all designed around the same Jungian research and, less directly, the ancient theory of four temperaments espoused and developed by philosophers from Hippocrates to Adler. All of them are extremely valuable in the understanding of human behaviour.

The model used here does not relate to any specific model currently on the market, but incorporates many ideas and insights I have gleaned through the years. I have called it the Behavioural Styles Model. If you are interested in studying this topic in more detail, there is plenty of information to be found on those models mentioned above and on the many others available.

Assertiveness and emotiveness

The BSM uses two broad dimensions to measure human behaviour—*emotiveness* and *assertiveness*. Let's start by having a look at each of these and defining their parameters.

Assertiveness
Assertiveness is:

> the degree to which a person asserts themselves and endeavours to influence the actions and opinions of others.

Assertiveness is all about how we interact with others: it is the degree to which we seek to press our opinions or to influence the behaviour, opinion and actions of other people.

- Highly assertive people are direct and to the point, fast, competitive, outspoken, dominant, and speak with authority and conviction.
- People with low assertiveness tend to be compliant, avoid risk, dislike confrontation, are cautious and ask questions rather than tell people what to do.

Most people we know can be placed at some point along this continuum from high in assertiveness to low.

Emotiveness
Emotiveness is:

> the degree to which we express our feelings and emotions and the way in which we relate to and interact with others.

Emotiveness is all about the way we relate emotionally to other people and the degree to which we display our emotions. Some people are extremely emotive—they cry not only at the end of the movie but during the ads—they are open and animated, relaxed, warm, informal, share their feelings readily and communicate both physically and verbally. These people are *high in emotiveness*. Other people are more self-contained and reserved. They avoid social interaction and rarely share their feelings and thoughts, they tend to favour structure and procedure and lack animation and physical contact—these people are *low in emotiveness.*

Two dimensions, four behavioural styles

If we overlay these two dimensions of human behaviour we end up with four very different behavioural styles:

	Assertiveness	
	Low	High
Low	Low assertiveness Low emotiveness	High assertiveness Low emotiveness
High	Low assertiveness High emotiveness	High assertiveness High emotiveness

(Emotiveness)

In order to remember these four styles more easily we have given each a name:

	Assertiveness	
	Low	High
Low	Thinker	Driver
High	Feeler	Enthusiast

(Emotiveness)

In order to use this information about human behaviour to your political advantage within your organisation, it is important to clearly comprehend each of the four behavioural styles and how each interacts with the others.

Let's have a look at each of the four styles and outline the behavioural characteristics for each.

Driver—high assertiveness, low emotiveness

Drivers are people who like to get things done, to produce tangible, bottom line results. They like to be in control and often establish very strong power bases within the organisation. Relationships are of little value to them, except in a professional, hardline sense where they can contribute to the achievement of goals. While they do not have a strong focus on detail, they expect others to substantiate their claims and to explain how their ideas will contribute to bottom line results. Drivers are very independent, preferring to work on their own and manage themselves. Their demeanour is 'cool' and 'distant' and they have little tolerance for expressions of feelings. Organisation is one of their strengths; they are competitive and work quickly to achieve their goals.

Strengths   The Driver's predominant strength is their ability to get fast results. They are highly assertive, direct and at times blunt, cutting through the niceties to get to the real issues. Their ability to rise above the details and focus on the big picture allows them to see the effect of individual actions on the bottom line.

Weaknesses   Like all of the behavioural styles, the Driver's weaknesses appear in direct response to their strengths. They can often seem abrasive and insensitive to the needs of others—their concern for results causes them to treat people as machines and ignore personal requirements. Consequently, people can see them as rude and arrogant. Sometimes their failure to give sufficient attention to detail can cause problems.

Behavioural characteristics

Results driven	Goal oriented
Bottom line focus	Prefers to be self-managing
Competitive	Low tolerance for feelings
Strong willed	Decisive
Likes control	Cool and distant
Likes action	Dominant
Problem solver	Accepts challenges
Likes authority	Fast
Good organisers	High self-esteem

Thinker—low assertiveness, low emotiveness
Thinkers are those who like planning and performing tasks using specific methods and procedures. Information and detail are important to them and precision and care in completing a task are extremely high priorities. When faced with making decisions, Thinkers will gather large amounts of information to enable them to make the most objective decision possible. Their preference is to work alone and tend to avoid personal interaction wherever possible. They dislike a lack of order and avoid surprises at all costs.

Strengths Thinkers are invaluable when it comes to tasks that require detail and precision; they have the ability to amass copious amounts of detail and to solve complex problems. They embrace tasks that are tedious and boring and persevere until the task is completed. Thinkers are well organised and efficient.

Weaknesses Thinkers are often too task oriented and are slow and painstakingly given to detail by nature. They tend to be slow decision makers, always seeking more information before finalising. Often they appear to be cold, aloof and impersonal because they put so much emphasis on facts and rationality. Their bias towards perfectionism often brands them as pedantic and tiresome.

Behavioural characteristics

Cautious	Avoid personal contact
Slow	Organised
Serious	Like structure and procedure
Persistent	Perfectionist
Disciplined	Seek facts and information
Precise	Good problem solvers
Like detail	Work well alone
Diplomatic	Critical of performance
Accurate	Pedantic

Feeler—low assertiveness, high emotiveness

Feelers place a premium on close relationships, trust and loyalties. They care for the wellbeing of those around them and always consider the personal impact of change, offering support and assistance. They are warm, friendly and sociable people concerned with the emotional comfort of others. They will spend much time supporting the team and ensuring harmony is maintained, providing a steadying and calming influence in the workplace.

Strengths The Feeler builds long-term, constructive relationships—they are willing to conform and to support the team and its leader. They make exceptional team members, taking on the caring responsibilities that are often overlooked or undervalued by the other styles. Thinkers make excellent counsellors providing a willing shoulder to cry upon.

Weaknesses As with the other styles, the weaknesses of the Feelers are an extension of their strengths. Sometimes they focus on relationships at the expense of the task and fail to do an adequate job. They are so sensitive to the needs and feelings of others that it can impair their ability to make objective judgements. They are slow to change and avoid decisions which might be uncomfortable or could generate conflict.

Behavioural characteristics

Relationship oriented	Loyal
Calm	Dependable
Good counselling skills	Supportive
Caring	Good listeners
Warm and friendly	Avoid conflict
Patient and considerate	Agreeable
Can gain support from others	Share feelings and emotions
Avoid risk	Ask many questions
Respectful	Consistent

Enthusiast—high assertiveness, high emotiveness

Enthusiasts are extremely social—they love to mix with people and get them on side in order to get the job done. They don't differentiate between work and play, and they ensure that work involves a sense of fun, excitement and challenge. They tend to have a creative approach to problem solving, have a great sense of vision and generally leave the implementation to others. They are highly achievement oriented and measure success by the acknowledgment, recognition and rewards they receive.

Strengths Enthusiasts' strengths lie in their ability to motivate and inspire others. They can quickly win people over to their ideas, getting them caught up in the drive to get the job done. They adapt quickly to change and are always full of ideas and suggestions (regardless of any lack of knowledge of the topic). Their creative nature helps them to generate useful options and alternatives.

Weaknesses Enthusiasts sometimes seem to be 'over the top', and their energy is often interpreted as insincerity. Their playful approach means they may lack depth and fail to be serious when necessary. They lack the ability to pay attention to detail and are easily bored by a repetitive or monotonous task. Enthusiasts find it hard to focus on one thing for any length of time. They have short attention spans and are easily distracted.

139

Behavioural characteristics

Visionaries/dreamers	Spontaneous
Persuasive	Talkative
Exaggerate	Sociable
Fast	Risk takers
Gregarious	Friendly
Undisciplined regarding time	Emotional
Optimistic	Enthusiastic
Motivate others	Inspirational
Intuitive	Self-focused

Who am I?

Start your journey to a better understanding of human behaviour by studying, and intimately understanding, the characteristics of your own behavioural style. Uncover one of the systems mentioned previously and establish your personal style more formally. However, in order for you to establish a 'thumbnail' view of your personal style, consider the list of behavioural characteristics below and highlight those you consider to be most like you. The section in which you find the most words highlighted is likely to be your dominant style. Remember that this is an unreliable and unsophisticated method for identifying your style—you *will* need to seek a statistically verifiable instrument to do it correctly. However, it will suit our purposes for you to have a rough idea of where you are coming from.

Once you have identified your dominant style, remembering that everyone has all of the styles to varying degrees, you can begin to observe the behavioural characteristics of others and to determine their dominant style. For example, take Roslyn and Michael in our story just prior to this section. Roslyn was highly assertive and, focused on getting results, she dragged Michael into her office and 'told' him what he should do. She was very direct, sharp and to the point. Based on these behavioural characteristics, we might conclude that Roslyn's behavioural style is that of the Driver. Michael, on the other hand, was more people oriented; he

Thinker		*Driver*	
Cautious	Avoid personal contact	Results	Goal oriented
Slow	Organised	Bottom line focus	Prefers to be self-managing
Serious	Likes structure and procedure	Competitive	Low tolerance for feelings
Persistent	Perfectionist	Strong willed	Decisive
Disciplined	Seeks facts and information	Likes control	Cool, distant
Precise	Good problem solver	Likes action	Dominant
Likes detail	Works well alone	Problem solver	Accepts challenges
Diplomatic	Critical of performance	Likes authority	Fast
Accurate	Pedantic	Good organisers	High self-esteem
Is relationship oriented	Loyal	Visionary or dreamer	Spontaneous
Calm	Dependable	Persuasive	Talkative
Good counselling skills	Supportive	Exaggerates	Sociable
Caring	Good listeners	Fast	Risk taker
Warm and friendly	Avoids conflict	Gregarious	Friendly
Patient and considerate	Agreeable	Undisciplined regarding time	Emotional
Can gain support from others	Share feelings and emotions	Optimistic	Enthusiastic
Risk avoider	Asks many questions	Motivates others	Inspirational
Respectful	Consistent	Intuitive	Self-focused
Feeler		*Enthusiast*	

cared about the impact of decisions on individuals, was less assertive, less directive and focused on maintaining harmony and avoiding conflict. Michael's behavioural style might be that of the Feeler.

141

Cast your mind back to Bernard and Zu. Bernard was conservative and quite introverted, ordered and pedantic, felt more comfortable with a spreadsheet and statistics than he did in the presence of people, and was not given to overtly expressing his feelings or emotions. These behavioural characteristics indicate that Bernard's behavioural style is that of the Thinker. Zu was flamboyant, outgoing and spontaneous. He enjoyed being around people and liked being the centre of attention—creative, expressive of his feelings and emotions, with a short attention span and no mind for detail, Zu is probably an Enthusiast.

It is not always so easy to determine an individual's behavioural style—not everyone is quite so typical in their behavioural characteristics. Over time, and with lots of practice, you will become far more proficient in this area. Let's look at how these four styles interact, and how to use a knowledge of them to your political advantage.

Adapting your personal style

The real political advantage of understanding behavioural styles is that you can become a *corporate chameleon*. The skill of the chameleon lies in the fact that they can camouflage themselves by adapting the colour of their skin to the surrounding environment, thus escaping their predators. While you may need to do this to avoid the clutches of those predators who practise negative politics, for those practising positive politics, there is a far more positive spin. Chameleons are all about *adaptability*, *versatility* and *flexibility*. As you practise positive politics, you can utilise your knowledge of behavioural styles to adapt your personal style to that of the people with whom you are dealing.

Benefits of being a corporate chameleon include:

- *building better rapport*—people feel most comfortable with those who reflect similar preferences to themselves

- *establishing relationships faster*—the socialisation process demands we establish common ground and you can achieve this faster by understanding a person's behavioural style and personal preferences
- *being more effective with more people*—our personal preferences ensure we give attention to those whose preferences are most like our own, and an understanding of behavioural styles helps us appreciate the preferences others and consequently establish more effective relationships
- *tailoring your communications*—each behavioural style prefers different communication styles; understanding this enables you to achieve greater 'cut through'
- *meeting personal agendas*—behavioural styles uncover dominant personal agendas, so you can adjust your behaviour to ensure people get what they want from a relationship or interaction
- *improving communication*—changing our personal communication style to better suit that of others provides clarity and enhances results.

Jim and Bill

Jim was a manager of a large team of about 150 people who formed smaller teams fulfilling five or six major organisational functions. Jim's behavioural style was predominantly that of a Feeler. He liked to have harmony in the workplace and avoided telling people what they should do or how they should manage their people. He disliked confrontation or conflict, was not particularly assertive and, where possible, sought consensus. He knew the business well and had been very successful in making his department function effectively.

The manager of one of his major teams, Bill, was a very strong Enthusiast in his behavioural style—and this was causing Jim some problems. Bill failed to appreciate the amount of detail required to do the job effectively, he offered too few working parameters to his people and consequently they were not meeting productivity demands.

He was a very loud and flamboyant character who extracted great loyalty from his people and could get them to really pull the stops out when the pressure was on. He was, however, unreliable at times and often set a poor example for his team.

Jim had spoken to Bill about the situation on numerous occasions. He had explained what he saw as the problems, they had discussed possible solutions and Bill had gone away to think them through, seeking input from his teams on the areas that affected them. But nothing ever got done—productivity continued to suffer.

In desperation, Jim spoke to Fiona, a colleague who had some knowledge of behavioural styles and was able to give him some valuable advice. After Jim had explained the circumstances, Fiona pointed out to him that the basic problem was the way in which he was trying to communicate to Bill. As an Enthusiast, Bill's preference was for colourful and overt demonstrations of feeling and emotions. He liked emphasis and modulation in voice tone and animated gestures and movement. Jim's personal style as a Feeler dictated that when he spoke to Bill concerning problems, he was calm, spoke softly and quietly, didn't move around or gesture and set up the chairs so there were no barriers between them. The conversation was more of a discussion and Jim certainly did not 'tell' Bill what he thought of him and his management behaviour but rather sought consensus and agreement. Obviously, he was not getting through to Bill—his words were going in one ear and out the other. Fiona and Jim talked the situation through and decided on a course of action.

Next day, Jim called Bill into his office. He asked Bill to sit in a seat in front of his desk and started outlining what he saw as the problems. Jim was passionate in his expressions, modulating his voice. During his talk, he rose from his seat and walked up and down, gesturing and waving his arms to make his point. When he came to tell Bill that there had to be a significant change on Bill's part, Jim slammed both hands flat on the desk.

'Bill, this has got to change. You have to have better control!'

Bill sat transfixed during the entire performance. He had never see Jim act in this way. He concluded that the points Jim was making were extremely important to him and the entire department. He did wonder why he had suddenly become so passionate about this topic and thought it strange that he hadn't mentioned it before, considering it seemed so important.

'Jim, you have to realise that I was unaware of the importance of these issues to you and the company,' he said.

Jim thought, 'What the heck have I been saying for the last three months?'

'I will give it some thought today and draft a range of solutions. Could we meet tomorrow morning at, say, 8 to discuss the viability of my options?'

Jim could hardly believe what he was hearing. 'Ah, sure, yes . . .' He fumbled for his diary. 'That's great.'

'Excellent, let's get together then. I am confident I will have some positive ideas to discuss.'

'Thanks Bill, I'll look forward to it.'

Bill got up from his chair and as he was passing through the door he turned.

'Jim, one more thing.' Jim looked up from his desk. 'I love it when you get angry. You should do it more often.' Bill disappeared out the door.

By adapting his personal style, Jim was able to get the message of poor performance across to Bill more effectively. Previously, Bill just hadn't been hearing what Jim was saying, Jim's style as a Feeler was too mellow and 'grey' as far as Bill was concerned. As soon as Jim started to use some of the characteristics of the Enthusiast's style, Bill started to listen. Jim learned through this experience the value of adaptability—by mirroring or matching someone's behavioural style, you can improve communication and exert greater political influence.

145

> By mirroring someone's behavioural style, you can improve communication and exert greater political influence.

Behavioural mirroring

The principles of mirroring another person's behavioural style are really quite easy to learn. Because our own styles are so ingrained, the hard part is changing your style to mirror another. People who have a style similar to our own are the easiest to work, with because they have similar preferences—they are the people with whom, under normal circumstances, we would develop friendships. It is easy for us to establish common ground with people of like style— we seek these people out because we are comfortable with how they behave and because their preferences match our preferences. Those whose preferences are very different to our own are the people with whom we find it the hardest to make conversation and develop relationships. We tend to avoid such situations. Mirroring is all about observing the styles of others and consciously modifying our behaviour to mirror theirs. In this way, we help them feel more comfortable, build rapport and enhance communication.

Using the styles

Obviously the hardest styles to mirror are those the least like our own. Opposing styles (shown in Figure 15) have the most potential to create conflict and tension. In an organisational context, they represent the group of people you will find it hardest to influence or get 'on side'.

Without any insight into or understanding of the positive value of styles that oppose our own, each would typically view the other in the following ways:

- *Drivers view Feelers* as soft, caring, wishy-washy types who don't get a lot done and are too sensitive for their own good.

Figure 15 Opposing styles

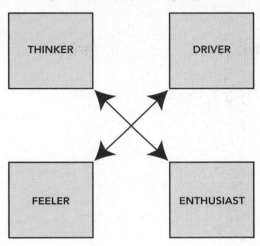

- *Feelers view Drivers* as arrogant, pushy, insensitive, uncaring types who chew people up and spit them out just to get the job done.
- *Thinkers view Enthusiasts* as loud, egocentric, distracting types who are too focused on having a good time and too shallow to actually be of any value.
- *Enthusiasts view Thinkers* as crusty, boring, colourless types who ask too many questions and are so focused on detail they get in the way of getting anything done.

Of course, each style is concentrating on differences and failing to see the benefits of each other's style. To gain the most from a relationship with a person who has an opposing style and to avoid conflict and tension you must try very hard to mirror that person's style. Table 7 outlines the types of behaviour you can use to mirror opposing styles.

Areas of common interest
Understanding the areas the styles have in common can also help you be more adaptable and consequently to maximise the political value of your relationships. Defining the similarities and using them to build rapport and uncover personal objectives will help you have greater political influence.

147

Table 6 Tactics for mirroring behaviour

Driver dealing with Feeler	<ul><li>show interest in personal things such as family, hobbies, personal achievements</li><li>share personal feelings and opinions</li><li>ask questions and seek consensus rather than telling them what to do</li><li>maintain a calm, friendly, pleasant manner</li><li>slow the pace down significantly</li><li>be casual and informal</li><li>show how your circumstances affects relationships or the team</li><li>guarantee reduced personal risk</li><li>offer personal assurances</li></ul>
Feeler dealing with Driver	<ul><li>avoid small talk; get straight to the point</li><li>have clearly defined goals</li><li>if you disagree, argue the point forcefully and with facts</li><li>ensure you are well organised</li><li>focus on results that affect the bottom line</li><li>be efficient</li><li>increase your pace</li><li>provide only relevant detail</li><li>don't present them with problems without having alternative solutions</li></ul>
Thinker dealing with Enthusiast	<ul><li>talk 'big picture', not detail</li><li>use visual aids, pictures, graphs or colour to make your point, not just figures</li><li>appeal to their ego, congratulate achievements</li><li>support their ideas</li><li>don't allow them to be sidetracked</li><li>move quickly</li><li>seek their advice</li><li>be direct</li><li>be more emotive; share your feelings and opinions</li></ul>

Enthusiast dealing with Thinker	■ provide lots of data
	■ avoid flamboyant presentation and explanation
	■ confirm conversations and agreed actions in writing
	■ provide tangible, factual evidence
	■ be accurate
	■ be prepared
	■ don't spend a lot of time on personal issues
	■ be well organised
	■ slow down your pace

- *Drivers* and *Enthusiasts* are highly *assertive.* They seek to strongly influence the actions and opinions of others.
- *Thinkers* and *Feelers* are low in *assertiveness.* They do not seek to influence the actions and opinions of others.
- *Drivers* and *Thinkers* are low in *emotiveness.* They are not demonstrative in the way they express their feelings and emotions in their relationships and interactions with others.
- *Enthusiasts* and *Feelers* are high in *emotiveness.* They are openly demonstrative in the way they express their feelings and emotions in their relationships and inter-actions with others.

Patricia and Colin

Patricia Wilmot sat in her inner city office pondering the complexity of her problem. It was 7 p.m. and outside a cold winter's rain had hastened the darkness, encouraging everyone to leave work early and lock themselves away in the warmth of their homes. As much as she would have liked to have done the same, Patricia knew she needed to make some decisions and develop a strategy before she permitted herself that luxury.

As head of research for Panavision, a large multi-national electronics manufacturer, she was the only

149

woman director. As such, she felt the need to continually promote the cause of women and to encourage greater equality in an organisation with a reputation in the industry as a bit of a 'boy's club'. She had a reputation for being hard-nosed and totally focused on getting the job done—getting it done better and faster than anyone else. Patricia could hardly be referred to as a 'warm' person. In fact, she often came across as quite cold and aloof. Patricia knew how people viewed her and the reputation she had developed, but she knew she had to not only survive but thrive in a man's world, and if this was the reputation that went with success, then she was willing to wear it.

She had spoken out at a board meeting a month ago about the need to increase the number of female managers in the organisation, pointing out the qualities that women managers brought to the workforce and the relevance of these qualities in the emerging 'new organisation'. There were a few muffled comments from the other directors, some rolling of the eyes and stifled coughs. Then the Chairman spoke.

'Patricia, I think you have a valid point.'

At 47, Brendan Myers was the youngest chairman to serve on the board. He was generally sympathetic to her views but at times she felt he still only paid lip service to many of the real issues. 'I have a situation that must be addressed,' he continued, 'and I would like you to set up a cross-functional team to develop recommendations for the board to consider.'

The task centred on the fact that new digital technology coming on line would necessitate the integration of many of the company's traditional product lines. Unless Panavision integrated quickly, and did it better than their competition, they would lose major market advantage and differentiation in the next two to five years. This was a complex problem from a technical perspective, however, the greatest challenge existed internally. The shift that Panavision was facing would threaten some of the traditional power bases within the organisation. Ultimately, some highly positioned and extremely successful line and product managers would be required to relinquish their authority to allow the integration to take place. For an organisation almost 35 years old, with an extremely entrenched culture, these changes were not going to come easily.

On receiving the brief from Brendan, Patricia didn't know whether this was a genuine effort on his part to raise her profile or whether he was actually setting her up for a fall. Either way, she was determined to ensure the team succeeded and fulfilled the task it had been set to achieve.

Patricia brought together the cross-functional team and for three weeks they had been working almost non-stop, gathering information and exploring options to present to the board. They had another two weeks before they had to present their preliminary findings and recommendations, but Patricia was striking a major problem. Team members were reporting that they were being 'sandbagged' in one major department and managers were refusing even to acknowledge their presence, let alone provide assistance. After extensively debriefing and grilling the team, she was able to eventually get out of them the name of their key antagonist and the nature of the barriers that had been placed in their way.

The main problem was one of the most senior managers, Colin Street. Patricia was not surprised—of all the senior managers, he certainly had the potential to lose the most. He did, however, have enormous influence in the organisation and if she was to have something substantial to present to the board in two weeks' time, she was going to need his help and support.

As Patricia sat in her office, the rain lashed violently against the windows. Recently she had been reading about behavioural styles and how an understanding of them could help to shift political situations to your advantage. If there was ever a time when she needed that sort of help, it was now. Patricia decided to write what information she had about Colin on her whiteboard and, from there, hopefully come up with a workable strategy that would turn the situation to her favour. She started to write.

Colin Street—GM Telecommunication

Personal		
48 years old	15 years with company	9 in current role
Part of the 'old boy' network	Top performing division due to mobile sales	Has received huge profit share in the last 5 years
Plays golf with Brendan	Doesn't relate well to women	Very good operator
Won the $80m account in '95 that solved major financial problem —hero	Second largest division behind computers	Very comfortable in his role—mate of Brendan
Really knows the telecommunications business	Lacks big picture understanding of how all aspects of the business will interlock In the future	Division is flagging a bit due to poor forecasting of the impact of overseas players in the market
Views on integration		
Definitely threatened	Would downgrade his status and probably his earnings	Would rather ignore the need to integrate
Cannot see the impact in the next 5–10 years	He will be retired— won't be his problem	Withholding vital information from the team
Political situation		
Strong power base —division's performance consistent	Has Brendan's respect and consequently his ear	Respected by all board members —well connected
Uncomfortable dealing with me	Lacks insight into macro company issues; narrow focus and knowledge	

Personality		
Lots of energy and enthusiasm	Can really get the job done	Fast paced, hard to tie down
Loves a drink with the boys	Tells lots of jokes	Does not indulge in a lot of small talk
Seems quite cold and calculating at times	Short attention span	Good at developing networks
Well liked by his staff	Loud and extroverted	Motivated to get results
Sets goals and achieves them	Has burnt out quite a few good staff members	Very positive—a real dreamer
Competitive	Dominating	Loves a challenge

Patricia stood back from the whiteboard and perused the information she had written down. 'OK, enough data, let's pull it all together into some sort of strategy.'

The Strategy	
What's the objective?	To get Colin Street on side, so he will not only provide the information we need, but support the major recommendation. Harness his political power and positioning to my advantage—gain leverage from it.
Situational overview	Doesn't really understand what is required for integration to succeed; feels his power base is threatened, is consequently defensive and protective—we must have his support!
Barriers	Is uncomfortable with me (women in senior positions in general, I think?!), does not see the need to support a change, could get Brendan to support his view over mine.
Behavioural style	Mix between a Driver and Enthusiast, but with the Driver dominating just slightly, especially in the work situations I have experienced. Both styles are very strong.

My behavioural style	Driver mainly, with a fair bit of Thinker thrown in for good measure. Means we are very alike in the driver area, but very different in the Thinker vs Enthusiast area.
Implications	As Drivers, we are likely to clash unless we have common objectives. He has a 'healthy' ego that is being threatened at the moment, sees the possible changes affecting the bottom line of his division, his competitive nature registers me as the enemy, losing control would also be a big concern to him. He would see my Thinker as being boorish and pedantic—better try to be more exciting?!
Actions	■ Talk to Colin about his 'sandbagging' the idea and why ■ Seek his support to win him over—bring him up to speed on the major and most workable recommendations ■ Arrange meeting with Brendan and bring him up to speed on the major and most workable recommendations ■ Explain how Colin is 'sandbagging' the idea and why ■ Arrange a meeting with Brendan, Colin and myself over a boardroom lunch—seek Colin's 'advice' and in so doing obtain his support (hopefully!) ■ Establish common goals—show him how we think the new structure would work, get his input, get him to see himself as a key player in the new structure—win/win/win ■ Show him how he can extend his power base to include other areas ■ Get him to see the big picture, be inspirational and visionary—paint pictures of how things could look ■ Be less pedantic about detail and data when dealing with him ■ Get him to see our opposition as the competition, not me ■ Include one of the male members of the team in our meetings ■ See if we can get him to help with the board presentation.

Patricia stepped back from the whiteboard and considered the bare bones of her strategy. She felt positive. She made a note to call Brendan first thing in the morning. 'I think this might work,' she murmured to herself.

Quickly she copied the notes from the board and stuffed them into her briefcase. As she switched off the lights to her office she noticed that outside it had stopped raining.

This story shows how you might be able to use your knowledge of behavioural styles to turn a negative political situation to your advantage. There are no guarantees that Patricia's strategy will work, but by taking a couple of steps back and viewing the situation in terms of who the players are, where the major problems lie and the behavioural styles in play, at least she has gleaned further relevant information on which to develop a strategy.

A strong understanding of human behaviour through the BSM provides you with a 'power tool' to use when building a positive political environment. So, put away the blunt handsaw you have been using up until now, plug in your 'power saw' and start seeing the benefits.

Chapter 6

ORGANISATIONAL CULTURES AND APPROPRIATE POLITICAL BEHAVIOUR

MANOEUVRE YOUR WAY THROUGH THE OFFICE MINEFIELD

Wisdom is being able to view things from
a macro perspective and see how the
component parts fit together.

Edward de Bono

The degree of politics, positive and negative, in the workplace is determined by a range of factors including the personal ambitions of key personalities, the availability of resources, the management style of influential people, the effectiveness of communication systems, the level of structure and policy, the competitive nature of the business and industry, reward systems, opportunity for promotion . . . The list could stretch out indefinitely. In many ways, endeavouring to understand and navigate your way through all of these combined factors successfully is a little like trying to 'tip toe through a mine field'. Everywhere you turn, you are faced with another situation that requires a particular approach or delicate handling. Organisations are labyrinths of interpersonal inter-action, unspoken laws, rules and standards of behaviour, tacit values and beliefs. For most of us, organisations are complex and confusing environments when considered from a political perspective.

To maximise your potential and create a positive political environment for yourself, it is extremely important that you understand how organisations work. You will need to

156

be able to identify the types of behaviours that are expected of you and those your organisation and your department consider valuable.

Imagine being lost and confused in a large and complex maze. You don't know which way to go next; you are sure you have been down this path before, however, you don't know if the next turn will lead to a dead end. Now see yourself being lifted above the maze to get a bird's-eye view of the whole thing—isn't it amazing how simple the maze seems from this perspective?

In this chapter we will give you a model that will help you understand in broad terms how organisations work. It offers that bird's-eye perspective of your organisation, your department and even the team in which you work. This understanding will give you the insight required to modify your behaviour so that it aligns with the behaviours your organisation considers valuable and important. This will, in turn, increase your value in the eyes of your management. The model will also improve your interaction and communication with other departments, making you more effective and helping to establish joint goals and develop win/win/win strategies—which is the basis for practising positive politics.

Welcome to the corporate village

Human beings are, by and large, social creatures. We like to herd and crave social interaction and stimulus. As a result we form communities that have social structures and hierarchies, rules, laws, behavioural expectations, values, beliefs, standards, rituals, customs, traditions and ceremonies. This infrastructure is designed to provide a stable environment in which to live, to facilitate our technologies and to make us feel comfortable and secure. We know how it all works, we know what is expected of us and there are few surprises. To be part of the community, you are expected to conform to the often unspoken rules that govern social behaviour. If we understand and live within this behavioural infrastructure then we will be accepted as part of the community; we will even have the opportunity to gain some status and position in the social hierarchy.

Organisations are a microcosm of society. The goals and objectives of organisations may differ greatly from those of society but the basic workings remain the same. Organisations are communities that contain complex patterns of social interaction, expected standards of behaviour, rules, laws, values, beliefs, traditions, rituals, and so on. Like communities, organisations are full of political systems that must be negotiated if you want to succeed.

All of these things combine to make up the *culture* of the organisation and determine how people must behave if they are to grow and succeed within the company. *Culture* is to organisations what *personality* is to individuals. Culture makes an organisation what it is—it is the way things are done, it is the things that are considered important. Culture expresses a company's direction and purpose, shared interests and mutual obligations. If you really want to succeed, you must embrace the company's culture, its beliefs and values. You must be willing to emulate the types of behaviours considered *normal* and to abide by both the written and unwritten laws by which it is governed.

The radicals among us can probably feel the hairs on the back of their neck raise at the very suggestion of such notions.

Nothing ever changes by accepting what is, you have to defy these laws to make a difference, conformists never make a social impact . . .

I agree with all of these statements and encourage those who feel it is their calling to confront the *status quo* to do so with vigour. However, it is not always possible to do this and to develop a positive political environment at the same time. While we are morally obliged to stand up for what is right and to be true to our convictions when they are challenged, being the corporate rebel is all about conflict

158

and confrontation. Practising positive politics is all about co-operation and collaboration. It is difficult, if not impossible, to do both at once.

Remember doing an exercise in high school science where you poured a culture into a Petrie dish with a range of different media, such as dirt, milk or water, to see if it would grow? Some things caused no reaction but others started to grow something similar to those furry things that move around the back of your refrigerator. When an individual joins an organisation, it is as though they are dropped into the culture in a Petrie dish. If they have the 'right' qualities then they will grow. This capacity to develop and prosper in an organisational environment can be thought of as a person's 'fit' with the organisation's culture.

Your personal 'fit' with an organisation's culture is determined by how closely your values, beliefs and standards align with those of the organisation. To the degree that your personality fits the culture of the organisation you will feel comfortable with how it operates and the behaviours it encourages. If you are well aligned with the organisation, then there is a better chance that you will 'grow' and become a success in that organisation.

In a case where your personality 'fit' with the organisation is poor, there is little likelihood that you will ever gain the recognition or the success you want. Simply put, you do not value the same things, share the same beliefs or hold the same standards, so consequently your behaviour will be perceived as inconsistent with what the organisation believes is necessary to be successful. It's not going to work.

It is unlikely that a person with a poor 'fit' will remain with the organisation for very long. Think of your own experience, where you have seen someone join your organisation, seem out of place and stay only a month or so before moving on.

Ensuring there is a good 'fit' between your personality and the organisation's culture is extremely important and is ideally considered during the interview for the job rather than after starting work.

Dominant and secondary cultures

While each organisation tends to have one overall culture that pervades most of its activities, it is possible for it to have a variety of different cultures operating under the same roof. Often these varying cultures exist in different departments and are usually driven by professional disciplines or functional demands. For example, one culture may exist in the accounting/administration area while another type may exist in the creative/design area. It is also possible to have different cultures based on the organisation's hierarchy—executive management may have a different culture to middle management, who may have a very different culture from those on the shopfloor. The overall culture of the organisation is the *dominant culture* and cultures that are peculiar to departments or hierarchies are *secondary cultures*.

When using the Organisational Cultures Model (OCM) outlined here it is valuable to consider not only the culture of your organisation as a whole unit but also the culture of your department or team and any others that you interact with on a regular basis.

By understanding the dominant culture of your organisation and the secondary cultures that exist in other important areas you will be able to determine the degree and nature of politics you are likely to encounter. It will also provide you with the insight required to modify your behaviour in order to maximise your political effectiveness in different situations.

Organisational Cultures Model

As with all models, this one provides a broad perspective on organisations and makes generalisations about certain professions, industries and behaviours. Before you start writing letters of protest explaining the inadequateness of the model, remember—it is only a model. If your organisation doesn't fit perfectly into the model, don't be surprised. Look for trends and general truths that can apply to your situation and synthesise the information through your personal knowledge and experience of your organisation.

When I was a boy I read a lot of comics. Before the days of sophisticated children's television, video and computer games, Superman, Phantom, Flash, Wonder Woman, Caspar, Richie Rich and Archie kept me enthralled. Often at the back of the comic, a range of novelty toys purchasable via mail order were advertised. Most of the merchandise advertised was fairly *passé* to a seven-year-old, except for an amazing item referred to as 'x-ray specs'. These special glasses enabled you to see things that other people couldn't see, for example, straight through a person's clothing. As a pre-pubescent youth, this seemed like a wonderful invention. I pondered the claims of the 'x-ray specs' long and hard, their obvious virtues and the possible disasters—what if you looked at your sister by accident?—but never plucked up the courage to place my order.

Think of the OCM as a type of 'x-ray specs' for organisations, which will allow you to see your organisation with greater clarity and in a way that you have never seen it before. Once you put on your 'OCM specs' you will begin to see the behavioural descriptors at work in the organisation and its different departments and divisions.

Structure and control

Let's start by considering the culture of organisations against two dimensions—*structure* and *control*.

Structure
When we refer to structure we mean:

> *the degree to which the organisation is reliant upon formal systems and procedures in order to achieve its goals and objectives.*

Structure is about detail, following procedure, developing policy, having written guidelines for behaviour, going by the book, methods for recording activity, going through the right channels, obeying the rules. It is a measure of an organisation's commitment to establishing and using a range of systems and procedures designed to provide structured and clearly defined parameters for effective operation. In its purest form, structure restricts any movement or flexibility outside written, agreed guidelines or set procedures. Using this as a dimension of measurement, organisations can have either a high degree of structure or a low degree of structure.

Control
Control is:

> *the degree to which the organisation provides direction and dictates the actions of its employees in order to achieve its goals and objectives.*

Control is about strong personalities and leadership, one-way communication, unarguable directives, authority, power, restriction of individual action, rewards for specific behaviours, selective distribution of resources, seeking to please a limited number of individuals. It is a measure of an organisation's commitment to the empowerment of its workforce and the degree of effective teamwork taking place at all levels of the organisation. In its purest form, control ensures power and decision making is retained at the most senior levels of the organisation. Using this as a dimension of measurement, organisations can have either a high degree of control or a low degree of control.

Two dimensions, four cultures

By overlaying these two dimensions we end up with four different cultures as outlined in Figure 16. In order to help us remember these four cultures more easily we have given each a name, as shown in Figure 17.

Each of these four cultures can, and often do, exist together in the one organisation. Every organisation has all four cultures to some degree. This model reflects human behaviour and as long as people (and not computers alone) form organisations, each cultural style will be evident to some degree.

Figure 16 Four organisational cultures

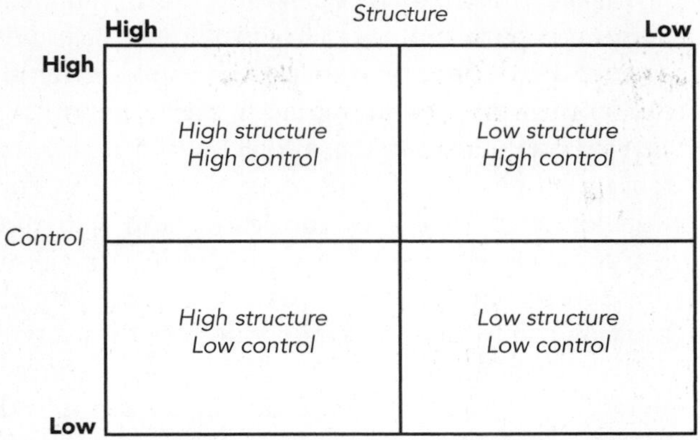

Structure

	High	Low
High Control	High structure High control	Low structure High control
Low	High structure Low control	Low structure Low control

Figure 17 Naming the four cultures

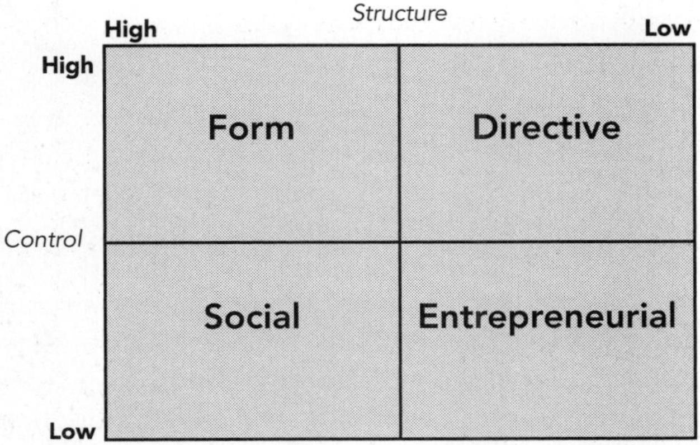

Structure

	High	Low
High Control	Form	Directive
Low	Social	Entrepreneurial

Let's now look at each of these cultures individually.

Directive culture—low structure, high control

Directive Cultures have dominated organisations since the Industrial Revolution but have become the focus of many change initiatives over the last decade.

Characteristics and values

Directive cultures are headed by strong, dominant leaders with charismatic personalities who provide a clear vision and purposeful direction. The leader is the source of wisdom, inspiration and authority and places high demands and expectations on staff, pushing them to achieve but also recognising their accomplishments and contributions. This culture breeds high levels of loyalty to the leader and staff understand the importance of aligning with the leader's goals to ensure job security and career growth. Consequently, those who align with the leader are looked after, as they have put the leader's goals before their own. Directive cultures are usually hierarchical in structure and decision making is done at executive levels then passed down the line to the staff. There is little participation and involvement of staff, except to fulfil the leader's directives. Often incentives, authority, job security and working conditions are used as a currency to control behaviour. Rewards and punishments are administered at the leader's discretion.

Strengths

Leaders of organisations that embrace a Directive culture have the ability to provide for their staff an extremely clear vision and direction. This causes individuals within the organisation to combine their efforts and focus effectively on the goals and objectives of the leader. Strong direction reduces confusion and conflict in the workplace, minimising the opportunity for individual agendas to be pursued. Directive cultures allow for high levels of responsiveness and quick decision making to meet changing market conditions. The leader's wisdom and knowledge is often used as a tool for winning new business and providing leverage where influence is required. There is often a positive personal relationship between the leader and the people and a sense of movement and achievement usually pervades the organisation.

Weaknesses

Leaders of Directive cultures carry the sole responsibility for providing the organisation with vision and direction. This precludes others from being involved in this important activity, leaving the organisation open to the possibility of the leader being misdirected, misinformed or personally inflexible when change is required. Staff in this culture are conditioned to be dependent on their managers' decisions and directions. Often leaders of Directive cultures are authoritarian in their management style, using threat and fear as motivators, and are prone to impulsive decisions and interventions that disrupt systems, plans and procedures that have been put into place. Due to the fact that most decisions are made at the top of the organisation, leaders are often burdened with so much work it slows down the processes and is a hindrance to the work of staff below them. There is also a tendency for these leaders to be 'hands-on' in their approach, which can cause confusion and inefficiency and a focus on short-term thinking rather than long-term strategy.

Political climate

Directive cultures are usually a hotbed of politics—undue energy is directed into 'playing the game' rather than getting the job done—due to the disproportionate level of authority held by the leaders and executive management. Staff in this culture are extremely aware of the need to 'curry favour' with the boss, who is prone to cultivate favourite staff members and to dispense gifts or curses at will. Managers who have the ear of the organisation's leader often behave like privileged earls at court, assuming authority by association and dispensing orders often without justification. While the best political strategy in this culture may be to closely align oneself with the 'powers that be', it is also dangerous to develop too close an alignment—in case of the leader's demise. In this culture, everybody is trying to score points and not always for the right reasons.

Roslyn and Kendal

Roslyn Faulkner was the owner/director of a large chain of retail fashion stores for women. She was a 'self-made woman', having started the business from the garage of her suburban home, designing and making clothing at

165

night and over the weekend and running a single store during the day. With time, the business grew substantially and 15 years later boasted 73 stores nationwide.

Roslyn was a 'big' personality. When she walked into a room she filled it to capacity and then some. She was boisterous and friendly with all of her staff, on most occasions remembering their names and some detail of their personal and family lives. Roslyn *was* the company. Her senior managers were there to fulfil her commands and had little input or control of their individual areas.

In the last few years business in the rag trade had become more difficult, particularly in ladies' fashion. The market had fragmented and it was becoming increasingly difficult to maintain market share. In order to address this situation, Roslyn decided to employ a marketing manager to conduct research and provide input on the general positioning of the stores and possible future target markets. The day Kendal started, Roslyn personally escorted her around head office and introduced her to as many staff as she could find—it was a grand introduction designed to align Kendal closely to the owner and position her as an extension of Roslyn's power base.

Kendal, in her late 20s, with a hard earned marketing degree under her belt, had worked in retail before but not in women's fashion. She was confident she could get a handle on the business quickly and within a couple of months develop a marketing plan that, with time, could add real dollars to the bottom line. She approached her first month in the company as a consulting assignment, visiting many of the stores and spending time with the designers and planners as they projected the next year's range. The more time she spent observing what the company was doing, the more convinced she became that radical changes needed to take place.

There was a lack of alignment between the advertised image of the store and the range of clothing being sold. Designs for coming seasons appealed to a wide range of ages, confusing shoppers and making it difficult for the store managers to sell. The design team was a mish mash of ages and physical sizes and was allowing personal preference to be reflected in the product range. She was going to have to recommend some radical surgery to Roslyn if the company was to start gaining market share in its proposed target markets.

Eight weeks after starting Kendal sat in Roslyn's office, having presented a weighty marketing plan detailing the research she had conducted, the changes she was recommending and the rationale for each. She was pleased with the way the report had come together and knew that the professional application of her recommendation would see the company reap real financial benefits. Kendal was consequently dumbstruck when the first thing Roslyn asked for was her resignation.

'Kendal, you have obviously developed the impression that your role is to run this company. With your lack of experience in women's fashion and such little time spent in my company I am astounded at the audacity of this report and the recommendations it contains. I built this company from nothing 15 years ago, I own it, I run it and I intend to continue to do so. While you have sought my advice and input, you have not really grasped what this company is all about. So I think it is best we part company now.'

At once, Kendal could see what had happened. Roslyn did not really want a marketing manager—what she wanted was a person to endorse her own ideas and implement her strategies. It wasn't worth arguing the point; Roslyn was the owner, the folk hero and matriarch of the company—there was no way she would ever allow Kendal to implement her marketing plan. Without a word, she walked out of Roslyn's office, gathered her things and left.

Kendal had come face to face with the full thrust of the Directive culture. She was used to working in an organisation where her contribution was valued and her professional standing was recognised. In this situation, what really

167

mattered was ensuring that the personal needs and ambitions of the owner were met. Kendal, perhaps naively, did not read the political situation well and by presenting her report challenged the validity of Roslyn's work over the last 15 years. Having the nature of Roslyn's company pressed home so dramatically Kendal could only conclude that the culture of that particular company would not suit her personality. She did well to just 'walk away'.

Form culture—high control, high structure

Form cultures have focus on systems and procedures, reducing the personal power of individual leaders and subjecting all behaviours to structure and policy.

Characteristics and values

Rules, guidelines, laws and procedures for the smooth operation of the organisation are all clearly defined and documented to ensure everyone understands their responsibilities and exactly how things are to be done. Through this approach Form cultures seek to establish order, stability and control, providing protection and security for their staff. The organisation's structure, lines of authority, job responsibilities, accountabilities and performance measures are all clearly defined doing away with the need for personal control by a leader. Typically, Form cultures are best suited to stable business environments and have difficulty keeping pace in rapidly changing situations due to the bureaucracy carried about their necks. Leadership within Form cultures is more about the forming of policy and adherence to procedure rather than the establishment of vision and direction. While the development of strategy is part of the structural policy, it tends to make projections based on historical data rather than responding innovatively to customer needs, the market and competitor activity.

Management in this culture judges performance against documented job descriptions and discourages personal initiative which challenges the rules. Staff are rewarded for adhering to policy and obeying the rules. Clearly defined objectives, procedures and systems help to reduce confusion, limit uncertainty and minimise inefficiency. Consistency of performance and quality is ensured and, by limiting the use of authority, the abuse of power is contained.

Strengths

Form cultures provide for staff a stable and predictable work environment where performance expectations are clearly defined and measured. They provide structures, policies and procedures that are well designed, reducing the need to consistently 'recreate the wheel'. Confusion, conflict and disagreement are minimised through the provision of clear lines of authority, and well defined responsibilities provide security and reduce stress. Staff are protected from managers who might otherwise arbitrarily use their authority (as sometimes happens in Directive cultures). In a Form culture, staff have a greater opportunity to direct their energies to their work without spending time playing political games. The role of the leader is minimised and replaced in part by policies, rules and guidelines. Authority and responsibility are inherent in the structure of the organisation and large and complex structures can be effectively managed at a distance without direct supervision.

Weaknesses

Form cultures are in essence bureaucratic and are by nature cumbersome and slow to change. Organisations in which a Form culture is predominant are at a distinct disadvantage in the current business environment which is epitomised by discontinuous change. Many of the reporting systems and procedures of these cultures are designed to check and control staff due to low levels of trust for the individual. This makes procedures time consuming to maintain, and takes time away from productive work. The highly formalised structures of this culture lead to very little co-operation and integration between departments, reducing the opportunities for synergy. One of the more restrictive characteristics of the Form culture is that the strictness of the rules and procedures causes the staff to lack innovation and initiative.

Consequently, these organisations underutilise the creative talents of individuals. They also restrict individual autonomy and the use of discretion in situations where efficiency and effectiveness could be improved. People in Form cultures are treated as commodities to be harnessed and controlled— a very impersonal and constrictive work environment.

Political climate

Form cultures are theoretically the least political of all of the styles. The high levels of structure and procedure limit the ability of individuals to promote their own cases and 'bend the rules' to their own advantage. Because there are policy statements and documented guidelines for every situation, very little is left up to individual interpretation or discretion, so there is not much value in trying to influence management in order to attract favour. On the whole, Form cultures *are* generally less political, but anyone who has worked in an organisation with this culture (the public service, or one of the big six accounting firms, for example), would attest to the high levels of political intrigue that still manage to take place. The politics is different than that for the Directive culture, as it focuses on using or leveraging the rules to achieve personal gain.

Entrepreneurial culture—low structure, low control

Entrepreneurial cultures produce a work situation that is highly energised and focuses on creating a motivational environment. The vision is clear and everyone works towards a goal that is 'bigger than themselves'.

Characteristics and values

In Entrepreneurial cultures there is a feeling of being unique, special, as everyone works towards their common goals. Staff reap intrinsic rewards from this environment, such as job satisfaction, personal achievement, team ethos and sharing of common goals. In an Entrepreneurial culture there are very few rules—in fact, people are encouraged to bend the rules if the end justifies the means. The environment is typically fast paced, celebrating individual and team successes and always striving to grow and achieve more. There is a sense of urgency as people are energised by working together as part of a team. Generally people are self-managing, there is little supervision, goals are set and the expectation is to do what is necessary to achieve them. People typically work long hours without complaining—stress is a common factor in an Entrepreneurial culture. There is a fair amount of conflict among teams as a normal part of work life. It's generally not personal; people are willing to argue in order to ensure they achieve their best for the team. Everyone is encouraged to participate, it is easy to be heard and acknowledged, individuals have high levels of authority and autonomy, and are empowered to do what is necessary to get the job done.

Strengths

The strengths of the Entrepreneurial culture are obvious: the clarity of vision and goals provides a common point for all to rally around. Low levels of control make the management of people far easier, as they are considered capable of the task and allowed simply to get on with it. Motivation within this culture is internal rather than external. The job itself and the associated goals and targets provide a natural momentum and motion. Individual initiative is used to its maximum, people are asked to stretch themselves, be innovative and creative in the solving of problems and making decisions. Failure is viewed as an opportunity to learn. People naturally derive a high self-esteem from this culture, they have a specific role to play in the team, they can see the results and there is a sense of growth and progress. The Entrepreneurial culture is extremely flexible and can consequently adapt itself easily to change.

Weaknesses

Despite the many strengths of the Entrepreneurial culture there are also a number of serious weaknesses with which to contend. Because of the fast pace and high stress it is not uncommon for Entrepreneurial cultures to burn people out, resulting in high staff turnover. There is little discipline in the

171

area of systems and procedures, which results in the tendency to waste resources. Entrepreneurial cultures are, by nature, activity driven, which can lead to a short-term mentality and a consequent lack of strategic planning. Long hours and hard work often substitute for planning and strategy. External competitiveness is usually very high, which tends to make teams inwardly focused and unco-operative with other groups. The co-ordination and control of individuals and resources in this culture is particularly difficult—things move so fast it is hard to keep track of them. The culture is often ruthless, end goals being all that counts, and people are sometimes run over in the process—it's part of the game.

Political climate

Entrepreneurial cultures have very loose structures and decision-making authority is shared across many levels of the organisation, so, as you can imagine, politics dominate within this culture. In fact, political skills or the ability to develop relationships and influence people are considered both necessary and valuable. Often the degree of authority people have is not determined by their position but rather by their ability to gain trust and respect through competent performance and by exuding personal confidence. Because there are so few rules and structural guidelines, 'getting things done' through unconventional channels is considered a valued skill—the result is what matters in the end. Entrepreneurial cultures are not for the politically faint hearted; they often epitomise the 'cut and thrust' of organisational politics. Those who understand the principles and can play the game inevitably do well in this culture.

Scott and Nigel

Alison caught Scott just as he burst through the door of the sales office and was heading for the coffee machine. His bright red tie was askew, his hair was all over the place, briefcase in his left hand, his coat flung casually over his right shoulder. He looked a mess and it was the start of the day.

172

'Hey, Ali, why so glum this morning?'

Scott was the sales director of a major distributor of imported wines and spirits. He had been in the role for about four years. Thirty-two and single, it was his ideal job. The nature of the product meant he had to spend a lot of time in bars and nightclubs attending promotions and supporting client functions. Well, he really didn't have to attend, but he enjoyed the social interaction and met lots of people.

'Scott, I need to have a word,' Alison was looking rather concerned.

'Sure, Ali, what's on your mind?'

'Scott, there's a man in your office waiting for you, says he's an auditor.'

Scott looked like he had been punched in the stomach. The smile suddenly disappeared from his face, which had drained to a sickly shade of white. It wasn't that he had anything to hide. It was the process of making the auditors happy and digging up the required detail that made him feel physically sick.

'Oh,' was all he could find to say. Scott wasn't all that big on detail and he knew he was in for a couple of weeks of pure hell.

'Thanks, Ali,' he finally managed.

As soon as Scott walked into his office he knew this was going to be even worse than he had imagined. 'Good morning, my name's Scott,' he said to a man he found there. 'I believe you wanted to see me.'

'Yes, I was, I mean, I do. My name is Nigel. I'm from the Auditor General's Department.' Nigel was the archetypal 'accounting nerd'. Nothing he was wearing got any brighter than a washed-out grey and his glasses looked like props from the set of a Buddy Holly movie. Any sort of human interaction made him nervous, which indicated he would be ruthless and merciless when left alone with a set of figures. Nigel explained to Scott the nature of his mission and showed him the appropriate authority allowing him to request this information.

> 'OK, Nigel, tell me what you want and we'll start getting it together for you.' Scott could not believe the list Nigel produced. There were five full pages of requests for information. 'So, how long do you think you'll be with us?' Scott enquired.
>
> 'Shouldn't be longer than a month, I wouldn't think,' said Nigel, with a broken-toothed smile.

In this case, we see the intrusion of one culture upon another. Nigel has come from a Form culture, where policy, systems and procedures rule his life. He is more comfortable working with numbers and spreadsheets than he is interacting with people. When Scott is confronted with the intrusion of this culture the contrast is as between black and white. Scott operates within an Entrepreneurial culture that loathes structure and procedure and seeks to avoid its strictures wherever possible. When faced with the need to immerse himself in a Form culture for a month, Scott feels physically sick.

Social culture—low control, high structure

Social cultures are based on relationships and a common reliance that exists between the organisation and the individual.

Characteristics and values

A high value is placed upon the people who work for the organisation and great effort is made to ensure people do not feel like a number or a small cog in a large machine. People are friendly and supportive of one another, often going out of their way to help others, even those not in their immediate workgroup. Co-operation is highly valued, as are interpersonal warmth and camaraderie. Conflict is not common in this culture, however, when it does occur, it is resolved as a priority in order to restore harmony. A lot of time and energy is spent listening to and caring for others and generally making oneself available. There is a great sense of belonging among those who work in this culture—people work naturally in teams, appreciate each other and acknowledge each other's contributions. Communication in a Social culture is typically very good, as people are willing to spend time talking to each other and sharing information. Organisations that embrace the Social culture will often go out of their way to 'look after' a staff member in a time of need, even beyond company policy or the obligations of the employment contract. This, in turn, engenders very high levels of loyalty among staff, who diligently care for the organisation, its equipment, the quality of its product and its reputation.

Strengths

There are many strengths inherent in the Social culture, due to its focus on people and interpersonal relationships. People in this culture are generally managed well—their potential is identified and utilised effectively. High levels of trust and empowerment raise individual self-esteem, increasing job satisfaction and decreasing absenteeism and staff turnover. Teamwork in this culture is very effective, as priority is placed on working together to achieve common goals. Social cultures create an excellent environment for providing effective and caring customer service. This culture provides a terrific medium for good communication, since individuals are encouraged to spend time with each other listening and sharing information. This culture also encourages a strong commitment to decisions, due to the fact people are consulted before decisions are made. Social cultures are highly structured—roles, responsibilities and authorities are clearly defined and people are reluctant to encroach on others' 'space'.

Weaknesses

One of the major weaknesses of the Social culture is the absence of a 'results' orientation. While the environment is extremely warm and friendly and encourages support and co-operation, there isn't much urgency or focus on the completion of the task. For these reasons, the Social culture is the least common of the cultures, and is rarely found in business due to its lack of competitiveness. Often decision

175

making in this culture is slow, as those involved are looking for consensus. Conflict in the workplace is often not handled very well and can become more of an issue than it deserves. Because there is a strong emphasis on caring for people, often the needs of the individual are put before those of the organisation.

Political climate

As you can imagine, the political climate within the Social culture is very stable. The high degree of structure ensures that everyone clearly knows their roles and responsibilities, similar to the Form culture. However, the low levels of control in the Social culture leave a large amount of flexibility for discretionary use of authority. People are trusted and empowered, so it is possible to use personal power to influence others to achieve individual goals. Interestingly, this option is not often used by those truly steeped in the Social culture. They are typically too aware of the needs of their fellow workers and conscious of not offending people to set out to influence others strategically for their own gain.

Identifying your organisation's culture

It is not difficult to identify the culture that exists in your organisation. As you were reading through the descriptions of each of the cultures you were probably relating your organisation or department to one in particular. In the grid below you will find a summary of behavioural descriptors for each of the cultures.

First, choose your target. Do you want to identify the culture of your total organisation or your own department? With your target in mind, read through the descriptors for each culture and highlight those that best describe your organisation or department. Remembering that all of the cultures will be evident to some degree, identify the dominant culture by counting which has the most descriptors highlighted.

Form	Directive
- Clear objectives, responsibilities and authority - Highly structured: written policy and procedure manuals; many systems, procedures and processes - Limited individual decision making - Secure work environment and low stress levels - Slow to change and respond to customer demands - Low levels of trust of staff; initiative not encouraged - Minimal co-operation between departments - Individual talents and creativity underused - Reasonably low level of politics	- Dominant leader - Leader has favourites - Clear vision - Directive management style - Decisions made at top of organisation - Organisation moves quickly to meet customer demands - Lack of strategic thinking - Rewards and punishments - Hierarchical structure - Little involvement and participation - Abuse of power for personal advantage - Use of threat and fear - High levels of politics

Social	Entrepreneurial
- Relationships have high priority - People care, are warm and friendly, support each other; a sense of belonging - Harmonious environment with good communication - Contributions acknowledged and appreciated - Conflict not handled well - High levels of loyalty and commitment - Trust/empowerment of individuals - Not a strong 'results' orientation - Slow decision-making processes - Medium levels of politics	- Fast pace - Results and success orientation - Clear goals and vision - Strong team orientation - Not many rules and regulations - People work hard and long hours - Highly motivated environment - Low levels of control - High self-esteem - Adapt quickly to change - Tends to burn people out - Waste of resources - Extremely high levels of politics

Aligning behaviours

Now that you have some insight into the way organisational cultures work, you can use this information to your political advantage. So far, you have gained insight and wisdom into organisational cultures. You have taken a 'birds-eye' view of your organisation or your department and now understand some of the thinking behind how it works. When it comes to gaining political advantage from this understanding, the simple theory is:

if you want to succeed in your organisation then you need to emulate the behaviours that best align with its culture.

Imagine a person working in an Entrepreneurial culture exhibiting behaviours best suited to a Social culture. They would be run over in a minute. Consider a manager whose style is best suited for a Directive culture being given the task of managing an organisation with a Form culture—the stress levels among staff would be so high the company would need to employ a psychologist. These mismatches just don't work. To achieve a successful 'fit', your behaviours must align with those that best suit the culture of your organisation, providing you with the opportunity to gain greater influence and exert more positive political power. Management will recognise you as being valuable because you are supporting the things they consider valuable. You can be trusted to promote the organisation's culture and values. The male charted accountant in the City who throws 'conservative' out of the window, starts wearing bright clothes, grows a ponytail, disregards procedure and laughs in the face of policy is not going anywhere in any account-ancy firm that has a dominant Form culture. So, align your behaviours to those things considered valuable to the culture of your organisation.

The behaviours that best suit each culture are listed below. Once you have determined the dominant culture of your organisation, you can use this list as an indicator of best behavioural fit.

Directive culture

I am pleased to say that while there are still some managers who adopt a management style suited to the Directive culture, this culture is dying. Managers who have this style are dinosaurs bound for extinction. If you feel that you are in an organisation that truly has a Directive culture that isn't likely to change, you are probably thinking about how you can get out—and it sounds like a good idea to me. Directive cultures are not fun places to work, except for people who are complete automatons, or who have no real interest in their work and simply do it for the money.

Directive culture—the right approach

- Identify the vision and goals of the leaders and make sure your work is connected to these aims
- Be obedient to management requests and do as directed
- Be loyal and put the goals of the leader before your own
- Emulate a directive management style with those around you
- Gain access to as many resources as you can
- Use that access to resources to control people and gain better performance
- If you are a lowly staff member, do things that gain rewards and avoid things that attract punishment
- If you are a manager, use rewards and punishment to control staff behaviour
- Either learn how to play negative politics—because it is rife in this culture—or brush up your curriculum vitae.

Form culture

The Form culture plays a very important role in corporate life. Often internal departments, such as finance and administration, have a Form culture which admirably serves other parts of the organisation, and without which it would be impossible for most organisations to survive. Some professions and institutions such as engineering, accountancy and hospitals adopt a Form culture as their dominant culture

179

because of the demands created by the mass of detail they generate. For other organisations, such a culture is better contained within specific departments.

Form culture—the right approach

- Be conservative
- Pedantically follow policy and procedure
- Don't buck the system—always do what is expected and play by the rules
- Never exceed your designated authority
- If in a position of conflict, refer to the procedure manual
- Utilise previous processes and procedures as benchmarks or precedents for future initiatives
- Stay focused on your responsibilities, only get involved in other projects if requested by management
- Be dependable and reliable
- Consistently meet deadlines, and provide requested work early when you can.

Nadair and Ryan

Nadair had worked for some pretty demanding bosses during his career but this new MD, Michelle Ryan, took the cake. Nadair was a senior partner in a high-powered firm of consultants specialising in mergers and takeovers. The pressures and demands of this sort of business were enormous, especially when the consequences of your decisions affected the lives of so many people. Nadair had just put the phone down after being 'summoned' (the only word he could think of to describe the threatening tone in her voice) to Ryan's office. It wasn't as if he didn't have enough stress to deal with—now he had to cop the brunt of her bad mood. He grabbed his pad and pen and headed for her office.

On the way, he took stock of his situation and gave some thought to where Ryan might be coming from. She had been in her current role for nine months and during that time had really turned the pressure up on all the partners, pushing for more volume and more margin from every account. All of his colleges were in the same boat, working 55 or 65 hours a week, spending little time with their families and passing their stress levels on to whoever happened to be around at the time. Ryan set high standards for herself and expected everyone else to match her. She was really a great manager, but her drive to succeed was almost an obsession. The effect this was having on the company as a whole was only now starting to show.

In the last three weeks there had been four resignations from highly placed people, who gave a wide range of reasons for leaving. However, rumour had it that the stress was getting too much and they had found greener pastures (with fewer hours) somewhere else. Nadair wondered how he would be faring in 18 months, and what the burnout rate would be. As he approached Ryan's office, he braced himself in preparation for his meeting.

'Nadair, come in and take a seat. Let's sit around the coffee table.' He took a seat reluctantly. Ryan was being cordial, which was unusual, so he expected the worst.

'How is the Williams and Murphy contract coming along? I hear that you have been working extremely hard to finalise the merger before the new financial year. I guess your children are wondering who the stranger is around the dinner table when you actually get there.'

Nadair was starting to feel a bit uncomfortable. In all of the meetings he had had with Ryan, she had never mentioned or asked about his family. In fact, he was surprised to find she knew he had one. As Ryan came from behind her desk, she pressed what the senior partners referred to as the 'magic button'—a remote for closing her office door. Myth had it that there were actually two buttons on the same remote, the one for the door, and one for a trap door leading to a shark pool. Now Nadair was really worried. Ryan continued.

'Nadair, you are one of the company's longest-serving partners and since my appointment you have shown great dedication and flexibility, as well as a measured insight into the personalities that make up the organisation. I have

181

come to rely on your judgements and take very seriously any suggestions you put forward. You are not a 'yes' man and I know you are not afraid to stand up to me if you believe what you are saying. These are the reasons I have asked you to this meeting. Nadair, I am concerned about the welfare of some of our key people. I am concerned that if they continue to bear their current workload they will burn themselves out in the next 12 months and their families and this organisation will lose both great parents and great colleagues. Frankly, I need your advice.'

Thinking back on this conversation later, Nadair was certain that he must have sat there for at least 30 seconds with his mouth hanging open. He could not believe what he was hearing. Ryan, for some reason still unknown to anyone, had come to the realisation that there was a need to provide some support mechanisms for those who were working so hard to achieve the company's goals and ideals.

Nadair formed a cross-functional team to address the need for cultural change within the organisation—the goal being to achieve results but within more realistic parameters. Ultimately, with Ryan's full support, the organisation embraced the concept of self-managing work teams as a means of sharing responsibility and spreading the decision making and problem solving across a broader base of people. Senior partners started to work in teams and seconded graduates from other areas as support. Senior partners began to assist Ryan in making the more important decisions for the company, giving them a sense of control over their own destinies. Their focus as senior partners switched to coaching and educating the younger partners, rather than doing all the work themselves. In the short term, this change increased operational costs by about 10 per cent per head; in the longer term, the organisation increased revenues by 15 per cent—and a recent attitude survey indicated that the staff satisfaction levels had improved significantly, as had productivity and efficiency.

Nadair's phone rang and his secretary answered. 'Hi Julie, it's Michelle Ryan here. Could I speak with Nadair please?'

'Nadair isn't in today, Ms Ryan. He has taken a rec day to be with his wife—it's their wedding anniversary.'

'Oh.' There was silence on the other end of the line. 'Could you leave a message at his home telling him I need to meet with him tomorrow morning at 7.30 regarding the Miller Brewery contract.'

'I certainly will.'

'Thank you, Julie, and by the way—send them both some flowers from us all, will you.'

'Right away, Ms Ryan.'

Entrepreneurial culture

Ryan and Nadair work in an organisation that has a high Entrepreneurial culture. The management and staff are driven to succeed and receive high rewards for their efforts. Unfortunately, the dangers of continuing at this pace are increased staff turnover and absenteeism, plus the burnout of valuable team members. Ryan was able to see the long-term dangers of continuing to push her people in this way, and with the help of Nadair and other senior partners, she was able to modify the culture by embracing some of the characteristics of the Social culture, achieving a workable balance. Unless those managing Entrepreneurial organisations acquire similar insight and balance, the ultimate costs to both staff and organisation can be very high.

In the current business environment, the Entrepreneurial culture is the one preferred by most organisations. With the need for organisations to achieve greater results, increased flexibility in meeting market demands and increased responsiveness to customer expectations—the Entrepreneurial culture is best suited to these conditions. However, this culture is a bittersweet pill. While there is much to gain by embracing it, there are major downsides. The tendency to have excessive expectations of staff, the waste of resources and the extremely high levels of politicking create an

183

environment of great stress and tension. For this reason, many organisations strive to balance it with a Social culture. More and more, the typical work environment is looking like the Entrepreneurial culture. This demands a change in management style as well as a change in the way people approach their work. While there are benefits for both, there are also pitfalls of which to be cautious.

Entrepreneurial culture—the right approach

- Be competent
- Develop a sense of urgency about your work
- Don't complain about your work load or the long hours you have to work
- Offer to take on extra tasks when the team has its back to the wall
- Always remain aware that you are part of a team
- Learn quickly, and don't make the same mistake twice
- Embrace change quickly—don't resist it
- Recognise and utilise the talents of those around you
- Only go into enough detail to do the task effectively
- Do what it takes to get the job done
- Be ruthless when necessary

Social culture

The Social culture does not feature much in western society due to its lack of focus on the procuring of results. Organisations that are focused on achieving bottom line results usually see little value in encouraging this sort of culture. There are some situations where the Social culture may be well suited as the dominant culture, such as in some volunteer organisations, churches and other government-backed social services. But generally speaking, few commercial organisations would hasten to embrace the Social culture as their dominant one. Interestingly, those organisations that embrace the Entrepreneurial culture should be looking to build their Social culture in a secondary role in order to provide some balance. Where the Entrepreneurial culture tends to overextend staff, the Social culture provides excellent support. A mix of the two, while difficult to achieve, certainly does seem ideal.

Social culture—the right approach

- Spend time finding out about your colleagues' social and family life
- Always allow time to listen to other people's problems
- Offer assistance, even if it is another team that needs help
- Focus on creating harmony, not conflict
- Co-operate wherever you can
- Treat people as individuals
- Acknowledge and praise individual contribution
- Communicate information openly and freely
- Support and commit to joint decisions
- Openly trust and empower others

A greater understanding of organisational culture will offer you advantages when it comes to developing a positive political environment. Use this information to assess your natural alignment within your organisation and department. It should be clear to you why there are instances when you clash with certain managers or are disciplined in regard to certain behaviours. You should be able to define the behaviours you need to embrace if you are to align with your organisation. Ultimately, you may decide that you are 'misplaced' and cannot make the changes necessary to achieve the career advancement you desire. This is also valuable information, as long as you make such a decision cautiously and rationally—not by gut emotion alone.

Chapter 7

SLEEPING WITH THE BOSS

ALL ABOUT SEX AND POLITICS

Be not too tame neither, but let your
own discretion be your tutor: suit the action to
the word, the word to the action; with this
special observance, that you o'erstep not
the modesty of nature.

William Shakespeare

Arnold seemed to have the knack to putting his foot in it every time he opened his mouth.

> **Arnold**
>
> A typical scenario: just the other day he came bursting into the office, stood in the middle of the floor, where everyone could see and hear him, and proceeded to tell a 'joke'.
>
> 'Did you hear the one about the Jew, the priest and the prostitute . . .?' At a single blow, he had offended just about everyone in the team. Mark, although a third generation Australian, is Jewish, and feels very strongly about his people and their suffering; Tracey is a practising and very dedicated Catholic; seven of the 12 people in our team are women. By the time Arnold had finished telling the joke, most of them had left or gone back to their work. The problem is, Arnold is kind of 'old school', and is not sensitive enough to understand how offensive this sort of thing can be.

Arnold committed the cardinal sin of being politically incorrect. That is, he acted in a way that was offensive to some, if not all, the people he worked with, causing them to feel uncomfortable or personally affronted. As we all know, such behaviour in the modern workplace can actually be illegal in certain circumstances, and people who are convicted of acting in a way that causes others to feel harassed are legally liable—as is the company for which they work. The topic we're addressing here is not harassment so much as political incorrectness. Rather than debate the important moral issues attached to this subject, we're going to restrict ourselves to an examination of the impact such behaviour can have on your ability to create a positive political environment.

Many people are feeling the pressure caused by the need to be *politically correct*. As our societies, and consequently our workplaces, become increasingly diverse this sort of pressure will only increase. In the past, subcultures such as ethnic or religious groups were generally small and contained, and rarely forced to integrate in large numbers. Men and women interacted within their gender groups—the men gathering to talk about sport, women and 'bloke'-type subjects down the pub, while the women sat around in their own groups at home or in another section of the hotel to talk about children, men and 'girl'-type subjects. Modern society is not like this at all. It demands far greater integration of all types of social, religious and ethnic groups. It creates an environment demanding considerable tolerance, sensitivity, respect and understanding.

Those who have trouble adapting to the sensibilities of this new work environment will find themselves at a political disadvantage. Their behaviour will put a lot of people offside and will diminish the amount of influence they can exert. Consequently, it is extremely important to find an appropriate balance and, if necessary, to *learn* the sensitivities required to relate effectively with a wide range of diverse individuals.

It is hard to address this topic without appearing to recommend that you allow your personality to fade to a light shade of beige. It may seem like you are required to be 'all things to all men' (or persons), in order to keep 'on side' with everyone, and so compromise your own character and worldview. This is not the case. Political correctness is about respect for an individual's personal position and proclivities, and about modifying your own behaviour to ensure the psychological comfort of others. This approach clashes with the notion many people hold that suggests, 'we are who we are and people just have to accept us the way we are'—which is often an excuse for an undisciplined tongue and diminished responsibility towards others. Somehow we need to find a balance between the two.

In your political environment, being politically correct is about developing and maintaining positive perceptions, enabling people to trust and respect you. Remember, trust and respect exist on the basis of reciprocity. If people believe that you understand their differences and respect their position regardless of your own, you in turn will receive the same respect from them. This will enable you to exert the political influence you need when required.

Political correctness is a question of balance and appropriateness.

Career Limiting Moves

The term CLM—referring to Career Limiting Moves—has become part of the vernacular in many of the organisations I work with. It is a term that has come to be synonymous with the actions or behaviour by individuals that make them look incompetent, immature, foolish or all three. CLMs are particularly problematic when such actions are observed by people in positions of power and influence, people who can affect the incline or decline of your career. The worst kind of CLMs are those that cause personal grief, embarrassment or discredit to the people to whom you report or those who can most influence your career success.

Nigel, Larry and Worthington

Nigel had a reputation for being the office clown. He was a nice enough guy, competent at his job—he just had a 'naughty boy' streak in him that drove him to play the occasional practical joke. Like the time the company's sales manager was on the showroom floor demonstrating a new product to a client and Nigel somehow got onto the paging system.

'Mr Matthews, Mr Matthews, a message from your mother. Could you please pick up a litre of milk and a kilo of carrots on your way home.' Tim Matthews was not particularly impressed, but took it as a joke.

One Friday afternoon, Nigel was distracted, bored and anticipating the coming weekend. He knew that Larry, his boss, was due to attend a regular management meeting in about an hour, so decided to play a bit of a joke on him. Every week, Larry took to the meeting a folder containing the weekly budget figures. Nigel stole into Larry's office when he was out briefly, and slipped a colour photo of a naked woman inside the figures folder. This would be a great joke. Nigel was intending to be at the water fountain near the boardroom so he could look through the windows and watch Larry's reaction as he opened the folder to read his figures.

Nigel positioned himself to watch for the reaction on Larry's face. When he saw Larry reach for the folder he started to chuckle. When he saw Larry hand the unopened folder to Graham Worthington, the company's church-going MD, you couldn't see Nigel for dust. He fell suddenly sick and left early.

When Nigel arrived at work on Monday, Larry was waiting for him and directed him straight into his office. Even though he had had the weekend to cool down, Larry was still fuming. Worthington had opened the folder and found the offending photo.

'Larry, is this some sort of sick joke?' he had asked.

Larry looked puzzled and vague. 'I'm sorry, Graham, I'm not with you.'

189

Worthington discreetly tilted the folder so that only Larry could see.

'What is this?'

It was now Larry's turn to feel ill. He knew exactly where the picture had originated. He made some lame apology. 'I'll talk to you after this meeting.' After the meeting Larry explained what he thought had happened.

'This boy needs some help,' Worthington had said. 'Ensure it was him who was responsible and, if it was, I want him in my office apologising first thing Monday morning.'

'So, Nigel, let's go see Worthington.'

'You're joking.'

'No, Nigel, Friday certainly was a joke, but *this* is no joke. Let's go.'

As you can imagine, Nigel found himself a contender for the big CLM award. He had seriously damaged the perceptions others had of him, his professionalism and his abilities. After this incident, the likelihood of him making quantum leaps in his career were very slim.

While Nigel's *faux pas* was of huge proportions, it is easy enough to allow small indiscretions to become CLMs. Consider the following CLMs and avoid them at all costs:

- impersonating the boss or talking about them in derogatory terms when they are standing in the doorway behind you
- arguing someone else's case when that person is a loser and has no respect or credibility—don't hitch your wagon to a stone
- associating with people who are troublemakers and adding minimum value to the organisation
- getting angry and expressing your emotions by abusing the people around you
- being blunt, rude or insensitive, and indiscriminately saying what is on your mind
- burning your bridges—build relationships, don't destroy them

190

- a 'scorched earth' policy—always try to contribute to other people's success, don't try to sabotage their success
- getting drunk at *any* work or business function—learn to control your drinking and consequently your behaviour, because many CLMs are made after a drink.

It takes a long time to recover ground after a major CLM. In some cases, you will never regain your credibility, or the trust and respect you have earned. For example, when I recently asked a friend about a business consultant I knew, she replied, 'I'd never use him, not after the way he handled that Johnson contract.'

She was referring to an incident that had occurred nine years ago. CLMs can really stick. Be careful.

Sex!

One of the most delicate issues involving political correctness in the workplace is that of sexual relationships occurring between consenting parties. It is a fact of life that where people interact there is and will always be the possibility of sexual chemistry. Many relationships are formed in the work environment, and it is only natural for a percentage of people who are interacting with each other on a daily basis to find some sort of relational compatibility. From a political perspective it is a question of how should you respond in a situation where you are, or would like to be, involved sexually with someone at work. What are the consequences, difficulties and pitfalls you are likely to face? And how can you navigate your way through this emotionally charged minefield?

The context of sexual relationships is really used here to indicate a level of intimacy that goes beyond simple friendship. Sexual relationships bring with them a whole universe of complexities that are hard enough to cope within a regular relationship, let alone in a situation where you have to relate to someone at work every day.

Making the decision to start a relationship with a person at work should not be taken lightly, because the ramifications

191

for both of you can be quite significant. This is not to say that such experiences are always negative, but there is always a change in the dynamic of a work relationship when it happens. Such a shift in relationships can significantly affect your political environment.

The couple

One theory is that the closer the person you are having the relationship with is to your workplace, the more disruptive the relationship can be to your ability to exert political influence. Say, for example, your partner works in a completely different department and you rarely cross paths during the day. Theoretically there should be little disruption or effect on your political environment. If the person works at the desk adjacent to yours, it is a completely different situation. The opportunity for disruption is extremely high and ultimately could change the perceptions others have of you both. Once again, this is not to say that it can't 'work'—it simply makes it more difficult. For these reasons you should take careful consideration before getting involved. The closer the other person is geographically positioned to you, the more care you should take with your decision to become involved.

Another theory is that you should never get involved in a relationship with the person to whom you are reporting. 'Never' is probably too strong a word, but the warning remains—be incredibly careful. In a boss/worker situation, a professional relationship already exists. There is a power base established that may come into conflict with the personal relationship you start to develop. Often these two very different types of relationships clash, usually over egos and familiarity. Intimacy allows for a breaking down of defences, a certain vulnerability on each person's part, so that when you move from the bedroom to the boardroom these newly gained insights can easily cause conflict and misunderstanding. Intimacy also presumes disclosure on both parts about many areas of a person's life—including work. When you have a relationship with your boss you usually gain access to information to which you would not previously been privileged. Using this information to your advantage could be perceived as immoral or at least unethical. If you are the boss, you are usually in a 'no win' situation—if you decide to withhold information it will put strain on the relationship in that important area of trust but if you decide to pass on information, you could be providing your partner with information from which they can derive advantage. You can't really win. Intimate relationships between boss and worker create a multiplicity of emotional dilemmas that can put a great strain on both professional and personal relationships. Such a situation can easily and quickly undermine any political influence you have developed and weaken your internal relationship network. The possibility of disclosure of sensitive information to the wrong people can put distance and chill into a relationship—both personal and professional.

If it is happening, if love is in the air and there is no way of stopping it, you need to precede with great caution and deliberation. Here is some sound advice from those who have 'been there':

- *Initially, keep it quiet*—for the first few weeks (but not much longer), it is best to lay low. Avoid any sort of obvious intimacy in the workplace, even having lunch or going home together. Don't let anyone know anything is going on. This can be extremely difficult, of course. Why? Well, what if this 'spark' you believe to be true love just turns out to be true lust and it goes out before it catches fire? If you keep it to yourselves at least for a few weeks, you'll have time to determine the nature of the relationship and where you think it is going.
- *Allow natural disclosure*—once you have both determined that there is some potential in the relationship going beyond a week, start being a couple. Occasionally have lunch together, attend work social functions as partners and if someone suggests something is happening between you, admit it, and respond with something

193

inane like 'Oh yes, we've been seeing each other for a while now'. This will stop the gossip quickly—once you admit there is nothing left to gossip about the conversation will quickly turn to something more interesting.

- *Announce it?*—if you can avoid the situation where you have to make a formal announcement of your new relationship, do. It is awkward and uncomfortable for everyone involved and projects your new relationship into the blinding and critical light of public scrutiny, which is the last thing anyone needs. However, there are some situations where announcing the fact that a relationship exists is the best thing to do, for example, where the CEO and a member of the executive team start a relationship. Rather than allowing rumour and innuendo to unsettle the team and cause a loss of business focus, it would probably be better to advise the team of the situation and disarm their fears and concerns. When you do make an announcement, expect the road to be a little rocky while everyone gets used to the idea.

The rule of thumb is to be discreet and conduct your relationship with maturity.

Work associates

Another important consideration is the impact your intimate relationship with the boss will have on your work associates. Your response may be 'it's none of their business' and, of course, you would be right in the personal sense. However, from a professional perspective, it can be very much their business. Your personal life is now on public display and those you work with could start treating you differently because you now have, or appear to have, a competitive advantage they will find hard to match. All of a sudden, you are in a 'privileged' situation, with a distinct benefit over everyone else.

Questions will be raised, such as:

- Do you have access to privileged information?
- Do you get told things we don't?
- Can you influence decisions unduly because of the relationship?
- Are my conversations with the boss still confidential?
- Are my conversations with you still confidential?
- Is this all above board and genuine or is it a political tactic?
- Will you get preferential treatment?
- Will you be allocated better work?

These questions must largely go unanswered—they are not the type of thing you actually bring up, are they? They lie just below the surface and are probably talked about by your peers—but not to your face. They are legitimate concerns. You can't avoid them and ultimately they could undermine the relationship you have had with your peers and weaken your political abilities and influence.

The outcomes could be:

- diminished trust—intimacy brings disclosure
- reduced credibility—the discovery that you have hormones
- decreased respect—confusion between personal and professional interests.

This is not necessarily fair or right, but you must accept such responses as legitimate and work extremely hard to prove that nothing has changed.

Roger and Anna

Amazon Creative Services (ACS) was a fast-moving advertising agency that dealt with the many and complex facets of media advertising. It was a socially interactive workplace and staff at all levels spent a lot of time together. The office contained a well-stocked bar that provided free drinks at any time of the day—it was housed in an area called 'The Play Room'.

Another aspect of the work was the high pressure everyone worked under to meet deadlines and keep clients happy.

Roger Hamilton headed up client services, which was basically the sales arm of the business. He had five high-powered and effective account directors reporting to him, who were responsible for generating the company's revenues. Roger was in his late 40s, twice married, twice divorced and currently single.

When one of his account directors resigned she was replaced by Anna, a very attractive European woman in her early 40s, ambitious and competitive both with her peers and in the marketplace. Her competitive nature caused a bit of a stir among the other account directors— they thought that Anna was not beyond using her 'female charms' to 'get her way' and that this gave her an unfair advantage. Particularly with Roger, as it seemed she was able to influence him significantly. Anna was single, recently divorced from her second marriage.

People around the office began to notice slight changes in the dynamic between Roger and Anna. It was very subtle at first—a familiarity, shared humour—and the account directors were taking particular notice, even starting to get concerned. Rumours of a 'liaison' were starting to circulate the office. It was at the regular Monday morning account directors' meeting that Roger made the announcement.

'I think it is important that you are all aware that Anna and I are seeing each other outside of work. I hasten to confirm that our relationship will have no impact on our work and certainly not affect the way this team has operated up until now.'

There was an uncomfortable silence. Anna met the gaze of her associates with a slight grin on her face. Just as Roger was about to go on, the silence was interrupted by Ty. He was a flamboyant Asian man, renowned for his ability to be disarmingly blunt. He had the knack of saying the things that most people would only dare think. It was suspected that Ty understood exactly what he was saying and the impact it was having on the listener.

'So, what exactly does this mean, Roger? Are you sleeping together?'

There were more than a few stifled snickers around the room and the grin disappeared from Anna's face. Roger rallied after a second's hesitation.

'Well, Ty, a characteristically straightforward question. Ah, I guess . . . well . . . yes, actually.'

Ty was not finished. 'Does this mean you two talk business in bed, when we are not there?'

At this the other account directors could not contain themselves. The room dissolved into fits of laughter while Ty was looking around in mock innocence.

Ty knew exactly what he had said. As things started to settle, Peter Dell, a long-time and very successful account director added his voice to the notion. 'Ty has actually raised an important point, Roger. This situation does put the rest of us at a disadvantage. We work in a competitive business and frankly this situation makes me feel uncomfortable.' There was a mumble of agreement from around the table.

Anna was no longer making eye contact and Roger was obviously a bit rattled.

'I can appreciate you feeling this way, however, Anna and I have discussed the implications of our relationship and have determined that we will in no way allow our relationship to get in the way of our professionalism. In the future, if you have concerns you must talk to me about them.'

When things go wrong

Personal relationships in the workplace are reasonably manageable when everything is going smoothly, but continued clear sailing is a rare phenomenon in most relationships. What about those mornings when you get up only to start the morning with a screaming argument? You get to work

197

and the tension is so thick you can cut the air with a knife. Everyone knows there is something going on, but no one can say anything. Worse still, what happens when one of you decides that what you thought was true love turned out to be just a little too much wine over dinner and wants to finish it a couple of weeks later? How do you go about dealing with the emotional turmoil that is associated with a relationship breakup when it is complicated by your professional relationship? Not very well, if past experience is much to go by. Breakups are usually associated with 'behind closed door' scenes, raised voices and often tears.

All of these things do not really help to project a consistent professional image and engender confidence, stability and respect. Next time you both enter a meeting, people will be wondering where the sensitivities lie, how fragile the fabric of the relationship is and how it will affect the decisions about to be made.

Once more, there is nothing *wrong* such relationships—just be aware of the minefield you are walking into!

The lust factor

So far we have been talking about intimate personal encounters that develop into something beyond 'just sex'. But what about those relationships in the office that are just about highly charged passion—pure sex. Relationships like this flare like magnesium, burn and die just as quickly as they started. This is 'the lust factor'. Such relationships have no depth and no chance of surviving, they simply serve a very short-term need for two individuals.

These relationships can be extremely damaging to a person's political standing. Passions and emotions run so high, and are so intense, that those involved often throw caution to the wind and become indiscreet in their behaviour. Consequently, they can become very public, affecting the perceptions people have of you—and not usually for the good. Your discretion comes into question.

Sprung, badly

In an interview, someone related a story about a manager and another staff member in their organisation who were caught up in a situation driven by passion and desire. The manager was a man in his late 30s, with a spouse and family, with a good career and prospects for advancement. The staff member was a young man in his early 20s who hadn't been in the organisation for very long. One Friday night, the team went out for drinks to a local hotel—as they often did. Between 8 and 9, people started slowly drifting off home. Around 9, one of the team headed back to the office to pick up some documents she wanted to work on over the weekend. Entering her floor, she heard strange noises coming from the photocopier room. On opening the door, she discovered the manager and staff member semi-clothed, in a passionate embrace. You can imagine the fallout from this incident. No official complaints or accusations were made, but the respect for and credibility of both of these people, particularly the manager, were shattered once the story was out—and it *did* get out. People found it hard to communicate with either of them and found it particularly difficult taking direction from the manager. Shortly after the incident occurred, the manager took a position with another company and the younger man was transferred interstate at his own request.

From a political perspective you can see how a single (if not necessarily momentous) indiscretion can seriously undermine a person's credibility and ability to influence—if not end their career altogether.

There are numerous similar stories any of us could relate where passion has overridden reason and someone has been tipped into hot water. If you are ever confronted by the lust factor, the best advice is—take a cold shower! Unless, that is, you are willing to throw away a hard-earned reputation and, perhaps, your career. You might get away with it unscathed and then again, the whole thing could explode in your face. Ask yourself—am I willing to take that risk? If so—go for it! If not, cool off!

The rules of the game

Here are few pointers for young players gleaned from personal experience (not all of it mine) and observation:

- Don't have sex in the broom closet—you'll get caught and how embarrassing will that be?
- Avoid obsessive behaviour—at home be as obsessive as you like, but at work, play it cool and act like a couple that has been together for 20 years.
- Don't spend every possible moment together at work—allow each other space.
- Don't drop all of your friends—you will probably need them again later.
- Avoid public displays of affection and emotion as a general rule—it makes people gag.
- Be scrupulously equitable in professional matters that involve your partner—it may even be wise to allow your bias to operate against them at times.

Surviving the morning after

So, you've both been to the work Christmas party, had a little too much to drink and allowed yourselves the indiscretion of shacking up in the local Travelodge for a few hours. You've had just that amount of booze that allows you to have great sex and to part without embarrassment with a 'Shee you at worksh t'morrow . . .' You wake up the next morning smiling about the dirty dream you had about so-and-so, only to find the receipt for the hotel bill and one of his socks sitting among the debris you left on the kitchen table after turning out your pockets at 3 in the morning.

'Oh my God . . .' Your hand is at your mouth and you suddenly feel very sick in the stomach. It gets worse. You realise that in a couple of hours you are going to have to turn up at work and face the music. What do you do?

This scenario gets a special mention, due to the gross awkwardness and sheer embarrassment that can result when 'it' happens. Some people couldn't give a hoot about fronting the person the morning after—most of us do. Here are some tips that might just get you through the morning:

- Feign sickness and get a doctor's certificate for a month's leave—by then your partner in sin will be wondering if it actually happened at all.
- Go into denial—'God only knows how those things turned up on my kitchen table but I *certainly* didn't do what I think I did.'
- Get to work early and lock yourself in your office.
- Act as if nothing at all happened—this is the best recourse, if you can possibly pull it off. Normality in this situation will breed confusion and your accomplice will start to wonder if it really was a dream: 'Well, where the hell did I lose that sock?'
- Deny, deny, deny. If someone walks up to you and asks 'Didn't you leave the party with so-and-so last night?', deny it. 'No way, it was probably Kylie, you know what she's like'. 'But I thought I saw you going into the Travelodge'. Again, deny it. 'You have got to be joking, how tacky! Better get new glasses, pal.' Unless they actually have photos of you in a compromising position, nothing can be proven. So deny, deny, deny!
- When they call (and they will!) what you do is going to be determined by how much you enjoyed and/or wish to repeat last night's performance. Regardless of your intentions, when they ask 'Did you enjoy last night?' your answer should be 'Look, I don't think this is an appropriate time to talk about it. I'll get back to you.' Then hang up. Now *you* are in control and you don't have to face it until you're ready.
- Avoid any one-on-one contact—cancel the meeting or take someone else with you, but don't put yourself in a situation where you have to be alone together.

At the end of the day, what you are really trying to do is buy some time to allow you to get your thoughts together. Who knows—this might be the love of your life. It could

201

also severely dent your otherwise pristine reputation and undermine your political influence. These precious commodities must be protected at all costs.

Non-consenting adults

There is a story that continues to circulate in industrial relations circles that we suspect falls into the category of an urban myth. It is, however, a good yarn that begs to be told. In the Industrial Relations court a barrister was cross-examining a manager who had been accused of sexual harassment by one of his female staff. They had gone to a business lunch with a few other people and he had had a little too much to drink, so the woman drove the manager back to the office in her car. She alleged that, during the journey, the manager had leant over and squeezed her breasts.

'Is it true that during the journey from the restaurant to the office, you leant over and squeezed Ms Smith's breasts three times?' queried the barrister.

'No, that is not true.'

'So, you deny squeezing Ms Smith's breasts three times?'

'Yes, I deny it.'

This dialogue went on for another 10 minutes until the barrister in frustration asked 'Well, sir, will you tell us exactly what did happen?'

To which the defendant replied indignantly 'I didn't squeeze them three times, I only squeezed them twice!'

As if that made a difference. Sexual harassment is sexual harassment whichever way you look at it. This sort of behaviour shouldn't happen, but it does. There is nothing that will undermine your credibility and political influence quicker than a sexual harassment conviction. Anyone working in a modern office environment will realise the seriousness of this situation.

- Don't make any unwelcome sexual advances to people in your work environment.
- Don't ever, in any way, force yourself sexually on another person.

No one can afford the stigma a sexual harassment charge leaves behind. Politically, it means disaster—your relationship network will collapse, your trustworthiness and credibility will be undermined, and your ability to gain favours will be minimised. It's also illegal and unethical. Just don't do it!

Speaking about political correctness and advising on appropriate behaviour all sounds very prudish in itself. If there is good advice that covers the situation generally, it would be:

Always err on the side of being conservative.

If in doubt—don't do it.

Chapter 8

DEALING WITH BEING 'DIFFERENT'

The best way for a women to get ahead at work
is to grow a penis.

Kathy Lette

While I don't think I'm particularly old in age or thinking, I am old enough to have witnessed during my lifetime a range of changes around me. Most obvious have been the amazing technical changes that have transformed every aspect of our lives, but of equal impact has been the social shift away from the predominant Anglo-Christian nuclear family unit towards a more multifaceted, multicultural society—a society influenced by many different races, religions and alternative lifestyles—making our social world a more colourful, sophisticated and interesting place to live. Generally we have become more tolerant, even accepting, of these 'invasions' of our comfortable Western worldview, embracing with alacrity many of the benefits such as the wonderful array of foreign foods, as well as certain festivals and rituals these changes have brought.

However, there are certain bastions of cultural resistance that find it difficult to integrate people and customs they consider 'different' from their standard. In a society that is aware of the need for equality and the need to recognise individuals on their merit, many organisations are still struggling with serious prejudices. Women *must* play an important part in the workforce—there is a real need for equality based on performance not gender. Varying ethnic backgrounds can add depth and insight if you look beyond cultural and aesthetic differences. The prejudice some people hold against those with 'different' sexual preferences can be damaging to the individuals involved and significantly affect organisational effectiveness. People with disabilities should not be regarded as 'commercially useless'.

Established commercial organisations, particularly, tend to harbour stereotypical models for success that discriminate against anyone who doesn't 'fit'. In most cases, these organisations are run by men—white, heterosexual and over 50—many of whom bring with them a long history of prejudice and discrimination. The good news is that these people are slowly being replaced by a new breed of executive that is more enlightened and who understands the need to embrace diversity. This is, however, a slow process. In the meantime, people who don't 'fit' suffer. Regardless of their ability and competence they are overlooked for positions, promotions and additional responsibilities.

Unfortunately, 'difference' often breeds insecurity and this can create a politically charged environment. The politics of being different in the workplace is no doubt the basis of a book in its own right. In this chapter I have chosen to focus on an issue of vital, if often unrecognised, importance to all organisations—the political differences women face in the workplace—with the intention of providing practical advice that many be transferable in some degree to other situations.

Venus versus Mars?

The role of women in the workplace is one of, if not the, most challenging issues that organisations and managers face in the next decade and beyond. It *must* be talked about, argued, discussed and challenged—over and over and over—until both sexes find the middle ground that allows the maximisation of the skills and talents inherent in each sex. This topic has gone beyond being a trendy issue on which to have views. As our economies, markets, societies and organisations change, it is becoming a competitive necessity to establish work environments that maximise the potential of talent, regardless of gender. Rosabeth Moss Kanter refers to this as 'meritocracy'—allowing talented people to surface, independent of where they sit in the organisation and regardless of the person's sex, race or sexual predilection.

Over the last decade we have seen significant progress in the achievement of equality for women in the workplace, but there is still a lot of room for improvement. Kathy Lette's tongue in cheek suggestion offered at the beginning of the chapter is pertinent, though I would suggest the situation is not quite that bad and that through the use of a range of tactics the situation can be significantly improved.

Part of my business for many years has involved working with groups of executive-level managers to improve communication and team skills. On many occasions this has revealed the kinds of politics that exist between men and women, particularly at senior levels. One particular workshop sticks in my mind as a poignant example of the subtleties and complexities of 'sexual politics'.

Marooned on a raft

We had been working for Tempo, a medium-sized property development company, for a short while. We were assisting their executive management team to assess the market position of the organisation and to develop strategies that would build their market share and provide a greater return on investment. Tempo had been in operation for 11 years, having been started by four male directors who had become disillusioned during time spent in large multinationals. Their vision was to start a company that was alive and vibrant, responsive to client needs and staffed by people who were dynamic and professional. Their vision had largely been realised, but there was a sense that they were becoming a bit stale and needed to rework their vision and move onto the next stage of growth. Traditionally, the property development industry has been dominated by men in management positions. Tempo was no different—the four company directors were male, although the last five years had seen quite a few women move into important management roles. When we started working with Tempo, there were four women and 10 men working at senior management level.

After spending time with this group, it became obvious

that they needed to work together more effectively as a team if they were to achieve their goals. So we arranged a weekend workshop to focus on these issues. One of the teambuilding exercises was called 'Raft Crossing', demanding that they were divided into two teams, given a range of material—drums, planks, ropes and so on—and set a complex task which included building a raft and traversing a substantial lake. Of course, there were certain parameters and a time frame within which they had to work to achieve their goals. Consequently the exercise required high levels of teamwork and co-operation for them to succeed. The group was divided into two teams of six, with four men and two women in each. My task was to oversee and observe one of these teams as they completed the task, which turned out to be a very interesting exercise indeed.

Things started off smoothly. Having been given the overall briefing, the team sat down together to read the complex and detailed instructions. They were aware of the basic competencies involved in the operation of a high performance team and the planning stage of the exercise went very well. It was in the implementation that things began to fall apart.

Jaquilin was appointed team leader. She had been with Tempo as marketing manager for three years and had succeeded through competence and hard work. At 32, Jaquilin was the mother of a very cute and very demanding five-year-old—most of the men she worked with found it a mystery how she coped with balancing a demanding career and a reasonably normal family life. They all watched her very closely to make sure she didn't 'trip up'.

Ruth was 30, single, and the company's management accountant. Her role at Tempo was outside the mainstream of property development and consequently veiled in mystique to a degree. She was treated as an expert in her field and really didn't pose a threat to those in the mainstream of the business.

The four men in the team were all significant players at Tempo:

James White—one of the original directors, aged 48, with 25 years in the industry.

Malcolm Rutherford—MD Commercial Property, aged 50, seven years with Tempo, 27 in the industry.

Hamish Glenn—MD Retail Property, 39, a young hotshot, four years with Tempo and only nine in the industry.

Nathan Silverwood—MD Domestic Property, 45, four years with Tempo, 20 years in the industry.

After spending significant time with all of these people I had found them to be extremely talented and ambitious, as well as highly intelligent and considered. They all held very important jobs and were aware of the need for the organisation to embrace modern work practices—which involved more prominent roles for women. What happened with the raftbuilding exercise was a parody of existing attitudes and practices in the workplace.

After reading the team's instructions, Jaquilin started to facilitate the team in identifying the tasks and allocating roles. At this point the team started to break up.

'I've built a raft before,' Hamish said as he jumped to his feet. 'Let's have a look at what we've got.'

The other men followed and started pulling apart the equipment. Jaquilin approached, saying 'Shouldn't we get some idea of where everyone's experience lies and then allocate tasks?'

'Yeah, I guess we should really,' agreed Nathan.

'Weren't you in the scouts, Nat?' James yelled out from five metres away. 'That means you should be able to tie knots, doesn't it?

'Sure does,' Nathan replied.

'Hey, alright, you're our man,' James was obviously impressed, 'Come over here and have a go at this.' Nathan was gone.

The four men were a hive of activity, assessing the equipment, testing different structural possibilities for the raft, checking out the best place to launch their craft . . .

Jaquilin and Ruth were literally left on the outer edge of the activity, watching. After about 10 minutes of this, Jaquilin made a gallant effort to fulfil her role as team leader.

'Guys, guys . . . GUYS!' They all stopped what they were doing and looked at her with bewilderment. 'We are supposed to be working as a team, with clear objectives, tasks and roles—there's no plan happening here.' The men looked at each other, obviously uncomfortable with Jaquilin's 'outburst', not to mention her desire to take some control of what they thought was a task best suited for men. What do women know about building rafts?

James rallied. 'OK, Jaq, we see your point. Get us organised.'

The team started to come together again. Jaquilin facilitated a plan, made sure that she and Ruth were included—it was definitely looking better. During this planning time, I observed some interesting behaviours. While Jaquilin was a very competent and confident manager in her own environment, among her peers in this situation she felt vulnerable and a touch anxious.

'OK . . . right. What next . . .?' Jaquilin was trying to think, on her feet, of the next best thing to do in facilitating the team. She was a bit nervous, and there were a few pauses. At this point, two interesting things happened. Firstly, all of the men were quiet. They let her stumble, allowed the embarrassing pauses to hang and refused to offer her any input. Secondly, after about 30 seconds of floundering, Malcolm asked, 'What now Jaq?', adding just a bit more pressure for good measure.

Jaquilin rallied and soon the team again set off about their tasks. Everything went better for 10 minutes and they returned to the rabble they were before. The plans were ignored, no one fulfilled their roles and Jaquilin and Ruth were left on the outer again as the men got on with the task. The women accepted what was happening as 'typical' and ended up sitting on the grass, chatting.

Eventually the men completed the raft. They were

running out of time and according to the rules they had to cross the lake with at least four people on the raft and return with a range of different materials from the other side. In a noble gesture, they tried to include the women.

'Come on, Ruth, you're on board.' Hamish was waving to come over.

'No way am I getting on that thing with you lot. I can't swim.'

'We've got life jackets,' Malcolm encouraged.

'No chance.' Ruth was adamant.

'OK, you're it, then Jaq,' Hamish had taken over as leader by the convoluted logic that his experience as a surf lifesaver made him the best choice.

'Hell, no, I saw Nat tying those knots,' she retorted.

The men didn't try any harder. Testosterone pumping, they were all eager to get out on the water and reach the other side. The plan was to use some improvised paddles to get to the other side and, when ready, to be pulled back by a long rope they had tied to the rear of the raft.

'Not a problem. You ladies can pull the raft back when we're finished on the other side. OK? Good. Let's go, guys.' Hamish was driving his team.

Much to the women's disgust, the raft was actually well made and remained together and afloat. The men got to the other side and gathered the required materials. When relaunching they left their paddles behind—time was short and they didn't need them anyway, since they were being pulled back.

'OK, girls, start pulling,' James ordered.

Jaquilin and Ruth were less than enthusiastic about the whole exercise and downright lethargic about the menial task they had been delegated as the men beat their chests and brought home the bacon—so to speak. They started reeling them in. When the raft was halfway across the lake, the men very excited about completing their tasks within the set timeframe, Jaquilin got a wicked glint in her eye.

'Hold up a minute, Ruth,' she said. They both stopped pulling.

'What's the problem?'

'No problem, but what would happen if we just stopped pulling?' Jaquilin asked.

'They would be stuck out in the middle of the lake with no way of getting back in.'

'Exactly,' Jaquilin threw down the rope. 'Let's go.' Ruth was shocked.

'You're joking!'

'No, I'm not joking. Those bastards treated us like we should be barefoot and pregnant in the kitchen throughout this entire exercise. Let them burn off their testosterone and find their own way back in.'

'But . . . James?' Ruth saw her career going down the toilet.

'Stuff James.' Jaquilin took Ruth by the arm and walked her away from the lake and back to the cabin where she poured them both a strong bourbon.

The men could not believe what they were seeing. A lot of noise was coming from the raft.

'Hey, what are you doing?'

'Come back, we don't have any paddles.'

'We're running out of time, we're going to lose.'

Eventually Hamish dived in and swam to shore, helping to pull the raft back in as the others tried to paddle with their hands. When they got back to shore they were tired, sore, depressed and pissed off. They had failed to complete the task in time—they had lost because of some emotional outburst on the part of the women in the team.

Debriefing the team about the exercise was interesting. We headed for the women's cabin. Things were tense and the team attacked the bourbon bottle as a diversion. At first there were sparks. The men felt let down. They couldn't understand what had gone wrong. Things were going so well. We were going to win. Then the women shared their feelings.

'I was supposed to lead that exercise, but you guys hijacked it from the start.' Jaquilin was angry.

'You were the wrong choice as leader,' Nathan said, putting his head in the lion's mouth.

'What the hell is that supposed to mean?' Jaquilin's eyes were lasers. Nathan tried to backpedal fast.

'Hey, I mean, no offence, but the task was really a male-type exercise, wasn't it?' There were mumbles of agreement from the men. Ruth wished she was somewhere else. I actually thought Jaquilin was going to get up and hit Nathan.

'This exercise was supposed to be about teams and leadership. We were supposed to co-operate and share information, develop a plan and work together to succeed—as a team. What it turned out to be was a parody of the sexual politics and the macho backslapping boys' club that Ruth and I and every other woman at Tempo has to put up with every day we walk into that office.'

The room had gone very quiet. They were either listening or working out who they were going to replace her with.

'You know why Ruth and I walked away?' Ruth was as interested to find out the answer to this question as the men were. 'Because we wanted to demonstrate how sick we are of the stereotypical bullshit we have to put up with.'

Jaquilin was right and I knew that her impassioned and impromptu speech had struck a chord. The room was silent. Time for me to step in and turn this into a learning experience—lucky me!

We talked around the issue for a good two hours as the tide on the first bourbon bottle and then another began to go out. After the first 15 minutes James interrupted me. 'Mark, as a Director I have to say that we are uncovering issues here that are of intrinsic worth to Tempo as an organisation. I think we should go and round up the other group and include them in this discussion.' We did; we explained the situation and began to grapple with the real issues.

Here's a summary of what this senior management

team learned from their experience and the parallels they saw with their workplace:

The men felt uncomfortable being led by a woman—they were happy to pay lip service to the fact that Jaquilin was the leader but, after listening to her instructions, went about doing their own thing.

They undermined her authority—subtly and unconsciously they went about ignoring her, negatively reinforcing her self-doubt and sabotaging her leadership role.

They replaced her with Hamish—he was male, had some perceived experience but most of all he was not a threat to their power base, as Jaquilin was.

They were supportive and attentive to Hamish as leader—he was a male.

They automatically saw the task in terms of traditional male and female roles—rafts, knots, risk, were all seen as 'male' territory. Ruth and Jaquilin were left out.

I asked, 'To what degree is management seen as male territory at Tempo?' The room went very quiet again.

This whole experience has come to epitomise for me many of the problems men and women are facing in the workplace. The politics between the sexes is so deep seated that I believe it is archetypal by nature.

Primal codes

During the debrief with Tempo we established that none of the men decided to exclude Ruth and Jaquilin from the exercise consciously. Their behaviour was motivated at subconscious levels which, from a positive perspective, meant there was no intent on their part, but from a negative perspective it meant that this happened 'naturally'—and that is scary. Some people might contend that the situation was the men's fault and that the need to change lies solely with them. It seems more complex than that. The problem lies with 'primal coding', which suggests that over the thousands of years of our evolution, men and women have been socially programmed to fulfil certain roles in order to ensure the

213

survival of the species. As we emerged from the agricultural era in the mid-1800s into the Industrial Revolution we brought with us our primal coding which involves men and women fulfilling very specific roles in society. In basic terms, these roles include women bearing the children and nurturing them through childhood and generally looking after the home. The men's role was to be the provider by going out to work and earning a living to provide for the running of the household. This primal coding has been burned into our subconscious over many generations—it is incredibly hard to change.

As we began to build large organisations men took the leadership roles, bringing with them the coding that clearly defined the roles women should play. Women were not 'supposed' to have careers within organisations, and if they did, those careers would not look anything like careers available to men. As more women entered the workforce and started to pursue careers, they typically ended up in areas not dominated by men—human resources, health and safety, communications. Women were not given the opportunity to operate in areas that had high levels of formal authority and control.

As we uncovered with Tempo, there is a strong belief that the words 'male' and 'management' are synonymous. Primal coding suggests (mainly to men) that men are better suited to management roles because of genetically acquired qualities. Because men were instrumental in the initial development of organisations, those organisations are structured to favour typical male behaviours. What if the tables were turned? It is interesting to consider how organisations might look had they been originally designed by women.

> # Don't deal with what should be, deal with what is.

So, organisational structures, culture and operations have been designed in the past to favour archetypal male behaviour, but now more women are coming into the workforce and demanding to be treated equally. Organisational cultures must therefore change to accommodate women. Not only that, men must stop seeing women as a threat to their power bases and egos, and understand the value and depth women can bring to the functioning of an organisation. Giving advice to a women's luncheon, Barbara Nokes, Advertising Executive with Grey London said, 'Don't deal with what should be, deal with what is.' Women must not see themselves as victims but start educating men to understand the changes that are taking place.

Things are changing, there is no doubt. Stereotypes are being challenged, both men and women are defying primal codes and establishing new rules, practices and behaviours. But, as we saw with Tempo and the raft exercise, it is extremely easy for us to fall back into our stereotypical roles without even realising it.

Five ways to succeed as a woman in the workplace

1. Refuse to conform to stereotypes: When the pressure is on for you to take the minutes at the team meeting—don't. As uncomfortable as it may get, wait for someone else to offer to do it. If you are continually asked directly to take the minutes you have a bigger problem. Speak to the most senior person who attends the meeting and point out this inappropriate request.

2. Maintain your gender: Sometimes the best way for men to ignore the fact you are a woman is to treat you as androgynous or, worse still, as a man. Hold to your identity as a woman and gently remind them of it if necessary—'Looking at this from a female perspective . . .' or 'Don't forget I represent our women customers . . .'.

3. Avoid being 'prickly' about stereotypical male behaviour: Some women are comfortable when men offer to open a door or pay for a meal. Others consider this another example of dominant behaviour. If you find this behaviour offensive, ensure you reject it in a kind

215

way—'Thank you but I can get the door myself', or 'I would be more comfortable paying my own share of the bill'. Remember, most men in these corporate situations are trying to come to grips with the new rules, and it is a process of education.

4. Don't be excessively aggressive: Firmly assert your rights as a woman but don't become known for being 'unreasonable' or 'difficult'. At times this may be a very hard position to hold, and in some cases, it may be totally impossible. However, trying to strike this balance is important.

5. Point out sexist behaviour: In many cases, men are not aware that their behaviour is sexist and demeaning to women. The education process is important, so, when a situation arises that is obviously sexist let those involved know exactly how you feel. Do, however, avoid violent outbursts of emotion and anger.

Sexual politics

Sexual politics involves using gender-specific idiosyncrasies to your political advantage. For example, in the Tempo case study there is a moment when Jaquilin stumbles, feeling unsure of her ability to lead a group of her peers. In this moment, the men were silent, didn't lend support or encouragement—in fact, Malcolm added to her pressure by negatively reinforcing her self-doubt. *'What now Jaq?'*—here we see the subtle use of sexual politics.

Coffee and tea is served in the executive boardroom. All of the men leave it on the trolley until one of the female executives gets up and puts it in the middle of the table. What is the underlying expectation? Serving the coffee? That's a female role, 'it wouldn't be appropriate for me, the Executive Chairman, to do that, would it?' Subtle pressure of this kind reinforces gender roles and undermines women's right to equality.

One of the boys

A high profile technology company, renowned for its innovative and fast moving product development, kept the pace up by establishing a SWAT team of their top guns. Individuals from across the organisation with a reputation for dedication, initiative and entrepreneurship were seconded into the SWAT Team with the brief to create the next generation of product and to 'keep making the waves, not riding them'. The team was famous for the long hours and weekends they dedicated to these creative meetings. The members of the team lived by the 'work hard, play hard' dictum, which led to heavy drinking sessions and the odd all-night card game. Research expeditions would take them all over the world in search of ideas and solutions. It was a standard joke that when you became a part of the SWAT team you kissed your partner and said 'See you in two years.'

For years this team consisted solely of men. That was, until Gloria Coulter joined the company. She joined the company when she was 28 and after a year was recognised as a high flier. Everyone knew about the quality of her work, and the results she got, particularly at executive level. When it came time to appoint a new member to the SWAT team, her name was at the top of the list. When her appointment was announced a ripple of concern went through the SWAT team.

Gloria was very excited. She knew that a stint on the SWAT team could guarantee her future, not just within the company but within the industry. She was determined to be incredibly successful. She had heard the rumours about the team and the sometimes unruly behaviour that was associated with their work. Gloria was not a prude by any stretch of the imagination and she knew she would be able to keep up with them in most areas.

It took Gloria a few months to settle in. The other members were wary and sceptical at first, but soon realised that Gloria could give as good as she got. She handled the long hours and the pressure of travel without a problem, but drew the line when the serious drinking started.

'Hey Gloria, you going to play cards with us tonight?'

'George, you know I love you and love spending time with you, but I have a husband and you know what? He's a darn sight better looking than you are.'

Lots of laughter.

'Good one, Gloria! See you in the morning. Don't forget we have to present on that robotics proposal at 10.'

'I'll be there, George—will you? See ya.'

It wasn't long before Gloria was accepted as a vital part of the team. After working with them for about 18 months, Gloria fronted a meeting with some earth-shattering news.

'Guys, I have some incredible news for you.' She had all their attention. 'We're having a baby.'

There was a stunned silence around the table until George responded.

'Gee, Gloria, I had forgotten you were a girl.'

As far as the guys in the SWAT team were concerned, Gloria 'fit in' extremely well. For 'fit in', read 'had emulated male behaviour to the extent that the guys felt comfortable'. This raises the question: for women to really succeed and rise to executive levels within organisations do they have to emulate male behaviour? In Gloria's case it worked, and it's likely that the sexual politics going on below the surface in a lot of organisations suggests just that. It makes sense, to a degree, that this should be the case. Many of the female executive role models have achieved because they have learned how to make it in a man's world, meaning they have been more 'masculine' than 'feminine' in their approach to business. One of the greatest compliments a male executive could give an aspiring female in the past was 'she's got balls'—the most hideous and sexist comment I know, but the measure of a female's suitability for management was the level of masculine behaviour she exhibited. Women were expected to shed their femininity to be a manager; it seemed that the two could never coexist. Such sexual politicking has caused much frustration, heartache and despair for many women. Hopefully we are now entering an enlightened era where the new organisation encourages equity, coexistence and a mutual blending of skills.

A blending of skills

Throughout this chapter we have discussed skills organisations expected from their managers in the past, and how organisational cultures have previously favoured men. What will the new organisation demand of their managers and where will men and women stand in relation to these new skill requirements?

Some theorists suggest that we will see a complete turnaround, in which new organisations will demand skills from management traditionally associated with 'female' primal coding. These same theorists contend that in the new organisation women make better managers than men, due to their natural abilities to nurture and to their 'greater sensitivity'. This sort of thinking only perpetuates gender differentiation. The reality is that the demands of the new organisation will put equal pressure on men and women to develop skill areas that may not come naturally to either of them.

Consider some of the skills required by managers in future organisations:

Vision / scenario planning	Financial analysis / interpretation
Strategic planning	Relationship networking
Interpersonal effectiveness	Information networks
Definitive decision making	Mentoring / coaching
Results orientation	Participation style
Concern for people	Interactive problem solving
Counselling	Team focus
Assertiveness	Influence
Leadership	Analytical listening
Creative / critical thinking	Conceptualisation
Cultural sensitivity	Facilitation
Multilevel communication	

Some of these skills are primal to men, some are primal to women, and some are new to both. I would suggest that we will see a blend of male and female skills and the mutual development of others. Embracing this concept defuses the male/female conflict, creates the need for mutual reliance and necessitates doing away with sexual politics altogether.

Living together

Developing harmonious relationships between men and women in the workplace is a bit like learning to live with the habits and idiosyncrasies of a new partner. It is essential to allow a lot of give and take, and to ensure each has the opportunity to get used to the other. There is no doubt that it is women who have faced up to the difficult task of integration first. However, there is a need for men to clearly understand the reasoning behind their prejudices and to modify their behaviour to ensure women are totally and successfully integrated into our organisations. In my research on this topic (including interviews with many successful women) I have uncovered a range of tips and advice, mainly for women, on handling the politics they face daily in organisations. I have included it with the view that it might help some.

- *Don't cry at work.* If you do your male colleagues will never forget it. Nokes suggests you try whistling instead, 'You can't whistle and cry at the same time.'
- *Don't try to drink the boys under the table.* A drunk female will be remembered and will incite more comment than a drunk male. Unfair, perhaps, but a fact of life.
- *Be a woman.* Remember the issues of image and presentation we discussed in Chapter 3. Dress appropriately—you don't have to be Holly Hobby, but you don't have to be Lee Iacocca either. Be feminine if you want to be.
- *Don't get mad, get better.* Nothing can replace enterprise and nothing will slow you down like resentment. Your

basic commodity is your ability to perform competently in your chosen professions. Keep getting better and better.
- *Communicate confidently.* Put your case strongly, whatever it may be. Research suggests that women are more likely to downplay their certainty than men.
- *Be assertive, but leave anger and resentment behind.*
- *Become educators within your organisations* because, in many cases, men are not aware what is going on, even within themselves—remember the Tempo experience—and many men are struggling to come to grips with the emerging new age women. The rules are changing and we are not sure what we are supposed to do.

Being a woman in the modern workplace will become an increasingly easier experience. Political manipulation of women by men will decrease as women become more adept at managing their political environments and men become more aware of the value of promoting equal opportunities for women. Women must keep pushing back the tide, forcing men and organisations to do what is just and right for women.

A word to men

Traditionally men are reluctant to come out too strongly on behalf of women in the workforce. It will appear to be a breach of brotherhood solidarity. A lot of men are so out of touch that they simply have no idea of the gross sexism they perpetuate. And some are actively seeking to establish equalities and recognise women for the great work they do.

My advice to men is this:

- Get behind the cause strongly: women will continue to fight for their rights so you may as well help them.
- Go beyond lip-service to the notion of equality for women, seek to understand the issues and embrace the benefits to be gained both personally and for your departments and organisations.

221

- Try to increase your awareness of the behaviour driven by your 'primal coding'. Seek to correct this behaviour in order to avoid offence and conflict.
- Never use gender as a means of political manipulation.

For both men and women it is vital to establish a foundation of positive politics, looking always for win/win/win situations.

To those who are different

To those of you who face the difficulty of politics in the workplace that comes with being different in some way to the norm—hang on. Things are changing, but the changes are by incremental rather than monumental steps. A critical mass is building in social attitudes and as the older, more conservative, directors or organisations are replaced by more enlightened, contemporary managers things will become more equitable. As the more traditional organisational structures and stereotypical roles diminish, so will the pressure that exists to conform and so will the blatant political environment such organisations generate.

My advice:

- Perform the basics well.
- Be confident about your abilities.
- Don't be ashamed of who you are.
- Don't be afraid to stick your neck out.
- If you are being politically manipulated—talk to someone in authority.
- Try to find a professional group that will support you and your different abilities or point of view.
- Know your legal rights and assert them when necessary.

When all is said and done, it is your right to be who you are and to live your own life without being disadvantaged in the workplace.

222

Chapter 9

NEGATIVE POLITICS AND HOW THEY WORK

CONTENDING WITH NEGATIVE POLITICS

Round about the cauldron go;
In the poison'd entrails throw . . .
Double, double toil and trouble;
Fire burn, and cauldron bubble.

Macbeth, William Shakespeare

This chapter is dedicated to everyone who has ever woken to find they have a dirty great dagger sticking out of their back—which, if you think about it, is most of us. Most of us have been the hapless victims of some act of negative politics. We have all at some time been manipulated, maligned, coerced, slandered and eventually gazumped, by the psychopolitical games practised by masters of the art of negative politics. These artisans loiter in dark corners whispering slippery words and incantations, stirring the murky cauldrons of rumour, innuendo and deceit. For the innocent, experiencing the full blast of one of their campaigns can be devastating. To face unbelievable accusations and to receive, through the 'grapevine', feedback on the things one is supposed to have said or done can be a frustrating, humiliating and angering experience.

Being forewarned is forearmed, as the saying goes, and if you are to contend with the dark activities of these people, then you must understand:

1. why they practise this art
2. what techniques they use to wound their prey
3. how to survive the onslaught of negative politics.

223

As explained earlier, (see page 10), negative politics is any action which, made with intent, adversely affects others to the benefit of the perpetrator. Such actions are carried out with the purpose of achieving personal goals, and by nature show disregard for the goals of both the 'victim' and the organisation.

Know your enemy

Those who practise 'the art' have one thing in common: they are all motivated by self-interest, and do not care about the hurt or anxiety their actions and behaviours cause others. They treat life as a competition and adopt a win/lose mentality that demands *they* must win at any cost. For these people, the fact that others lose or are devastated in the process is irrelevant, as long as they are able to achieve their goals and objectives. *The end justifies the means.* Some of them will do almost anything if it helps them get what they want.

Jamie

I had completed a paper the CEO needed to present to the board in New York. He called to say he was leaving for the airport at 6.00 a.m. the next morning. At 4.00 p.m. I left the paper with my secretary—the courier was due any minute. That night I received an angry call from the CEO asking where the hell the document was—it hadn't arrived. I hand delivered a copy to him at 11.00 p.m. after going to the office and printing and binding another copy. It wasn't till a year later (after the offender had left the organisation) I found out that the parcel had been 'stolen'— there is no other word to use—by a rival colleague who was annoyed that the CEO had asked me to prepare the paper and not him. He thought it would really make me look bad if it didn't arrive—it certainly did.

Another thing practitioners of 'the art' have in common is that most, if not all, of their political activities happen 'off stage'. Few of their practices are conducted or documented in a public fashion. They are played out in quiet conversations held in corridors, local cafés or behind closed doors. If their surreptitious activities are referred to, they are usually denied. The subtle nature of their tactics makes it very hard to pin them down: as someone said, 'It's like trying to catch a bucket of steam.' Consequently, trying to confront and resolve issues resulting from someone's political manoeuvring can be difficult and very frustrating—but it is not impossible.

Three approaches to negative politics

The apocalyptic horsemen of the Book of Revelations present a good analogy for those practising 'the art'. Each of the horsemen bore gifts of catastrophe and destruction, which they proceeded to unleash on the unsuspecting without fear or favour.

The Red Horse—'The power to take peace and create war'

Some individuals within organisations practise black arts from an innate skill base, subconsciously 'pointing the bone' to ensure they achieve their personal objectives. Often these behaviours were developed during childhood and have long been part of the individual's way of coping with life in general. These people don't necessarily know they are causing harm. They may be 'innocents', but the consequences of their actions are never the less concrete and costly.

The Black Horse—'The power to inflict famine'

There are others who perceive that the only way they will ever achieve success is through the strategic use of manipulation and coercion, and therefore they make a conscious effort to get their way by devious means. They see 'the art' as a tool to assist them in their rise within the organisation. Although many others are hurt along the way, they accept

225

this as an unfortunate but inevitable consequence. Often these behaviours stem from low self-esteem or a sense of inferiority. Rather than feeling comfortable with who they are and confident in their own abilities, these practitioners of 'the art' feel the need to 'load the dice' to help improve their chances of success.

If someone has to win then someone has to lose, and the laws of natural selection dictate to them that they are not going to be the one to lose. So, 'the end justifies the means' and if negative politics are required to ensure a win— negative politics prevail.

The Pale Horse—'Death was the rider and Hell followed with him'

The third category of person that practises 'the art' is perhaps the most frightening—those who are fully cognisant of the damage and emotional anguish their activities cause, yet persist in practising negative politics. Why? *Because they actually enjoy it!* While their motives remain basically the same as the other riders, their enjoyment adds a dimension of evil to their activities.

Wayne

I eventually went to his office and confronted him about the situation a week later. He put down his pen and crossed his arms. A wicked smirk smeared his face.

'I really don't know what you're talking about.' Naively, I reiterated the circumstances and made my accusation regarding his involvement, with the increasing feeling that my words were dribbling down my chin and dirtying my shirt front.

'I did hear some whispers about that, but are you suggesting that I was responsible?' I continued to explain how I believed he had instigated the rumours and the angst and hardship they had caused.

'That's a real shame, perhaps you should watch your back a bit more,' he said. 'But trust me, it wasn't me who started the rumours. Now I do have important work to do.' As I left his office, I looked back. He gave me a plastic smile and I thought—he actually enjoys it, he actually enjoys it.

Whatever the reasoning behind why these people get involved in negative politics, the facts are that they exist within every decently sized organisation and you will have to contend with them at some stage during your career. Understanding their techniques and having a strategy for dealing with them are crucial to your success, if not your ability to survive.

> # Never allow the politics of a situation to distract you from the importance of competence and professionalism.

Why people use negative politics

The reasons for practising the art of negative politics, or the purpose in behaving in this destructive way, lies buried deep within such people's core attitudes, beliefs and value systems. Let's have a look at some of the dominant reasons for such behaviour.

Lust for power, control and authority

This is a theme that dominates many of Shakespeare's plays. *Julius Caesar*, for example, gives us the famous 'stab you in the back', and 'you too, Brutus' analogies. Practitioners of the art have a need to bring somebody down from their perch, to rob them of whatever power and authority they have. They believe, as Shakespeare's Brutus did, that their opponent has accumulated too much power and authority, and needs to be 'dethroned' in order to restore balance and perspective. In most cases, the real aim of the exercise is to gain that power for themselves, or for the practitioner to be better positioned to benefit from any ensuing reshuffling and restructuring. They believe it is their right, if not their duty, to set things straight. Once again, the exercise usually centres around self-aggrandisement, personal gain and profit. Often in these circumstances the deeds are shrouded in the cloak of righteousness—'it's for the good of the company'.

The rationale is ostensibly that the actions are for the common good. But rarely is anybody fooled by such platitudes—the winners, and usually the losers, in these games are very clear. Underlying such acts is the basic need for control and authority, the need to be able to feed hungry egos and sagging self-esteem. Of course, the ultimate act in the practice of the art is to actually 'kill' your adversaries as we see with Brutus and Caesar, or Macbeth and Duncan. Modern parallels might be seen in such black personalities as Hitler, Amin and Hussein. In the workforce, the equivalent is to get someone sacked or to make someone's life so unpleasant through the exercise of negative politics that they are forced to leave the organisation—and it happens often enough.

Molly

I didn't really want to leave; I liked the company and the people I worked with. However, if I wanted to progress in my career, I had to. The bottom line was I was a threat to him—and on top of that, I was a woman. The quality of my work was such that he perceived it made him look bad. He did, on a few occasions, claim my work as his own, that was bound to happen, but he couldn't do that for ever. Once I started to be recognised as a 'rising star' by senior management the trouble began. My work was reduced to the mundane while special projects and high profile work were given blatantly to others. Rumours started circulating that 'the knives were out for me', he started being ultracritical of the work I did, and what's worse pointing out my supposed errors to his superiors. In the end, I became so hamstrung and so 'on the outer' that people were avoiding me and failing to co-operate with anything I had to do. I was bored, frustrated and unchallenged. It finally got too much and I found another position which, I might add, is better paid and carries greater responsibility. I don't know why I let him stuff me around for so long.

Raw, naked ambition

Who can forget Gordon Gekko and *Wall Street*, the movie that cut to the quick of a generation obsessed with winning and success, stood us back on our heels and made us re-evaluate our lives and our values—well, for a week, anyway. Greed is good, win at any cost, it doesn't matter who you burn along the way, there is always going to be a loser and you might as well make sure it's not you. We've all experienced the thick, salty taste of winning—the euphoria, the ecstasy. The thing is, for some, it becomes an obsession, going beyond the realm of decency and taking on the cloak of raw, naked, unbridled ambition.

At the core of their belief system is chiselled the precept, 'I deserve to win'. Winning is perceived as their right and 'how dare' anyone stand in their way. Being the best, having the most and wielding power are at the top of their list of values. Nothing is more important and no cost is too great in achieving these ends. These misconceptions can be launched from overinflated self-esteem, or a God complex that makes them see all others as lesser beings. Alternatively, and just as lethally, practitioners are motivated by an extremely low self-esteem that drives them to compensate for perceived inadequacies by always outdoing others. Either way, the behaviour ends up the same. Ego *is* a dirty word when it means the humiliation and emotional crucifixion of others.

Revenge

Revenge is another basic motivation of 'the art'—and to those who practise, revenge is very sweet indeed. Most of us hold the basic belief that those who do others wrong will

229

eventually reap what they have sown. We leave it in the 'lap of the Gods', as it were, and choose the solace that we have done the right thing. Those who practise 'the art' believe it is their responsibility to exact revenge on anyone who is perceived to have done them wrong. They take a very proactive stance and start rattling around in their grab bag for an appropriate curse to cast as soon as a supposed indiscretion takes place. The knives are out, the lines are drawn, the guns are loaded. And black art practitioners will watch and smile as you burn.

Kwan

'I just didn't know what had hit me. I was unceremoniously called into the General Manager's office and put on the carpet.

'You know that breaching the security of our client database is a serious offence?'

Yes, of course I did. The information was the core of our business and most of it extremely confidential.

'We have it on record that you have interrogated our client database five times in the last week. I want to know why you shouldn't be fired immediately?' I was literally dumbfounded. I couldn't speak and I'm sure my mouth was hanging open. Why shouldn't I be fired? Because I didn't bloody do it.

'Isn't your computer password protected?' Well, yes it is, but someone could have learned what my password is and . . .

In the end I wasn't fired due to 'reasonable doubt' (it was a law firm), but my loyalty from that time on was always in question. About a week after things had settled down, I was sitting in a coffee shop just near work. A colleague I had had a run-in with a couple of months before stood over my table. She slid a small piece of paper towards me, on which was written the password for my computer. With that she smiled and walked away. I felt sick. Needless to say I found a new job within a month. Life's too short to put up with that sh . . .'

Tools of negative politics

Those who practise 'the art' are incredibly resourceful. They have a wide range of tools at their disposal to use when attacking others to get their own way. Someone once said to me, after surviving a political attack, 'I never knew he was so devious or so skilful when it came to stabbing someone in the back.' Techniques are as diverse as they are devastating, and in this section we will analyse some of the more popular methods used in negative politics.

Voodoo

This is an outright attack on you as a person and is conducted from a distance. It could, and often does, involve slander as well as discrediting your work. The use of this technique can be blatant or subtle, depending what the practitioner considers will have the greatest effect. Consider some of these statements:

- 'Michael? You can't trust him to run a bath.'
- 'I've seen her work and, believe me, you wouldn't want to trust her with this.'
- 'I don't think it is appropriate for me to give my opinion of Peter's skills in this area.'
- 'Robert? Maybe . . . How important did you say this project is?'
- 'No comment.'

The degree of intensity may differ, but the technique remains the same—they take every appropriate opportunity to create an impression of personal or professional incompetence. Practitioners of 'the art' add a needle wherever they can, and make sure it is placed where it will cause the most pain and long-term discomfort.

Rearranging the goat's entrails

This 'skill' employs a range of methods you will no doubt be familiar with, but ultimately it is about manipulation. If there is one particular method black art practitioners enjoy employing over others it is the manipulation of people and events in order to achieve their premeditated outcomes. They do this by:

- openly criticising your work
- causing conflict between you and your boss or peers
- playing on your insecurities and weaknesses
- setting you up to fail
- feeding you inaccurate information
- getting you involved in tasks inappropriate to your skills
- taking credit for your work
- turning others against you.

These tactics can create a critical mass of opinion against you that will ultimately allow them to get their own way. Once again, these are all 'off stage' activities, usually taking place in the more casual settings of the corporate environment—in the canteen, before a meeting, over the coffee machine or around the photocopier. Comments are randomly slipped into a conversation and are usually shrouded by a 'genuine' concern for the company good.

Mario

'I knew something was going on when I saw him in the canteen having a cup of coffee with Margaret—he hates Margaret. His objective was clear in the end. There was a presentation scheduled where our project team was to outline the very positive outcomes of more than six months worth of research that would ultimately add significantly to the company's revenues. It was obvious that I would be the most likely person to make that presentation, considering my role as team leader. But he wanted to do the presentation and take the credit for himself. Systematically, he spoke to all of the team members, expressing his concern about me trying to take all of the 'limelight'. He also insinuated that some of my other presentations had been a 'bit off' lately and that it might be a good idea for someone else to take responsibility. There were a number of rumours circulated concerning my application for transfer to another department. Other situations occurred where I was made to look particularly incompetent. For example, I was told (by guess who) that a paper regarding the research was not due for another week. During that week I got a phone call from my general manager asking where the paper had got to—he was expecting it the previous Friday.

In the end he succeeded in developing a critical mass of feeling against me—to the point where one of the other team members suggested in a meeting that 'perhaps it would be better for another team member to make the presentation.' I was in a situation where it was futile for me to push my own wagon, but I would be damned if he was going to get the job. I had underestimated the hard work he had put in behind the scenes—the rest of the team was insistent that he was the best person to do the presentation. He was extremely clever, extremely clever. He's an exceptional chess player, you know! Not surprising, is it?'

Clever practitioners of 'the art' skilfully blend truth and lies. An outright barrage of lies and slander puts people on the offensive immediately. Practitioners, however, delicately balance the mix, taking great care to ensure that their lies are laced with just enough truth to make them credible. In the story above, the rumour that Mario was seeking transfer to another department was actually true, but the context in which it was used suggested that his loyalties were not really with the team—'so why should he make this most important of presentations, if he could be gone tomorrow?' People can use this technique because it is very difficult for others, if they don't have all the facts, to distinguish between the truth and distortion.

The Janus syndrome

This technique is prevalent among managers who are heavily involved in the practice of the black arts. Janus was the Roman god of doors and gateways, and also of beginnings. In the principal temple dedicated to Janus, there were two doorways—one facing east, the other facing west—and between them stood the god's statue, with two faces, one looking each way. Janus provides a most appropriate image for the art used when the practitioner is required to present one persona to 'those who count' and another to 'those they manipulate'.

Discussing this with a colleague, she asked in frustration, 'How can they [executive management] possibly let her get away with such behaviour?' The answer is that 'they' don't get to see what 'she' is really like. In board meetings and other interaction with 'those who count', practitioners present a balanced and sincere persona, saying and doing all the 'right things' to dazzle and impress. They express deep commitment to the modern management techniques that advocate teamwork, participation and empowerment. They can 'talk the talk' using all the buzz words, and sometimes they are even under the misconception that they practise them. But those who have to work with or under them know that the opposite is often true.

Ali

'I had this monumental fight with my boss just prior to both of us going into a meeting with her manager. It was all about power and control, her over me, and it was very dirty. Next thing, we were in the meeting with her boss and she was as sweet as pie. I couldn't believe what I was seeing. In a calm and positive manner she explained how important I was as part of her team. A most responsible and trust worthy contributor. That was a real eye-opener for me.'

The other face is the one seen by those subjected to their manipulative and subversive ways. If, by some act of misjudgement, you chose to discuss this problem with senior management, the reaction is likely to be cold, to say the least. The credibility of a disciple of Janus, in most cases, is very sound, and while there may be some awareness among management of 'indiscretions' used to achieve their ends, what they actually *know* about such activities is minor and generally ignored. It's the Janus Syndrome—the face *you* see is not necessarily the same face that is presented to others.

Other hexing techniques

Below are snapshots of some of the many techniques that feature in the grab bag used by those who practise 'the art'.

Bottomdrawing
When using this technique, practitioners ignore, or 'bottom-draw', ideas that are not their own. It is important that they are seen as *the* repository of all that is good and practical.

Topdrawing
The opposite to bottomdrawing occurs when the practitioner comes across a good idea and adopts it as their own—'topdrawing'. They rarely give credit to the person who originated the idea.

Turfguarding
This is the opposite to teamwork and resource sharing. Often practitioners guard their expertise and authority jealously, refusing to share it with anyone.

Haystacking
This occurs when your request for action or a decision of some kind is buried by the practitioner under other less important work. It can slow down your effectiveness and reduce your appearance of competence.

Information damming

To those practising 'the art', information is power and power is what it's all about. They are renowned for withholding information they think may give somebody else an advantage in any way.

Booby-trapping

This is part of the game of revenge that black art practitioners play. It involves 'getting even' with someone who has done them a perceived wrong by setting them up to look bad or to fail at a particular task.

Handgrenading

This a particularly deadly technique that is highly public and can be extremely humiliating. It involves 'lobbing' a live issue, such as a problem—personal or professional—you are encountering or a question you can't answer in your lap during a public meeting.

Sandbagging

When put in a situation they find unsavoury or not particularly to their liking, black art practitioners are often likely to 'sandbag'. That is, they will either ignore the situation or fail to co-operate in any way. The theory is, ignore it long enough and it will go away.

Brown-nosing

Most black art practitioners are consummate brown-nosers—we all know what that involves and see it happening regularly.

Surviving a negative political onslaught

Knowing the ways 'the art' can be practised is important, but protecting yourself against these devious techniques is an art in itself. Here we discuss some of the defensive techniques you can use when faced with these situations.

Gazumped!

Meet Suzanne. Mid-to-late 30s, single, well educated, competent, extremely ambitious, obsessive. Over the years she has earned the epithet of 'The Black Widow'— based on the number of people she has befriended, bled dry and eventually beheaded along the way. Her obsession is with power and control, and she will not allow anyone or anything stand in her way. As product manager for a medium-sized manufacturer of advanced communication technology, she has had a very successful career. She started with the company as a cadet straight out of university. She has progressed steadily through a range of important positions and is highly regarded by senior management as a valuable manager who can get results.

Martin is also a product manager for the same company and roughly the same age as Suzanne. He joined the organisation from a competitor a year ago and during this time has been able to establish himself as a competent and effective manager. While he is reasonably well connected within the organisation, he has not yet developed the contacts and confidences that Suzanne has.

At a recent management meeting, Martin presented an idea for the development of a new product he had been working on—one that would give the company entrance into a new and lucrative market. It would also align them more favourably with their major competitors and integrate a number of their existing technologies, expanding their potential and market appeal. While the investment required to float the idea was significant, the risk—at least at the outset—seemed viable. Those present at the meeting were positive, yet cautious, suggesting the idea warranted greater research—all, that is except Suzanne.

Suzanne's reaction to the idea was frigid. She found the whole concept ludicrous, not because the idea wasn't a good one, but because Martin's possible success in the venture could threaten her hard-earned reputation in the organisation as the rising star. She perceived that his success would mean her demise—so the knives were drawn.

During the meeting she maintained her composure, presenting a balanced approach to the pursuit of the idea, even feigning marginal support. Immediately after the meeting, she sidled up to Martin and complimented him on such an innovative suggestion. Yet by the time she emerged from the boardroom she had already devised a strategy that would bring Martin to his knees and his development proposal into disrepute.

The strategy was subtle and well planned. In the month leading up to the next management meeting she employed a number of well proven techniques. Firstly, she spoke to the other three product managers who were present at the meeting individually, discussing the proposal constructively but gently sowing doubt in their minds as to its viability and practicality. During this time she also spoke 'confidentially' to the Group Marketing Manager, who would ultimately take accountability for the project's implementation. She expressed her concerns about the credibility of the market research on which Martin had based his proposal and brought into question his loyalties—she had it from a 'reliable source' that he had recently applied for a position being advertised by their competitors.

The Group Marketing Manager said he should raise these issues with the General Manger of the division at golf on Sunday, and Suzanne said she would leave that to his discretion. The masterstroke in Suzanne's strategy was dealt to her hand by fate. A week before the meeting, the GM called her into his office and requested an informal update on a joint project that involved Martin, herself and two other senior managers. She advised him that the project wasn't going as well as it could, due to a hold-up on certain aspects of the plan under Martin's control. She didn't want to be critical, but she wasn't sure that Martin was really up to the complexity of the task.

Martin couldn't understand why, all of a sudden, everyone from the GM down had gone cold on his idea.

They all seemed so positive at last month's meeting! No one wanted to talk to him about it, but he certainly wasn't getting the assistance he expected.

At the next meeting, Martin's idea appeared on the agenda—briefly. It was raised by the GM, who made the comment, 'I think we should leave that idea for a while yet, Martin. You do have other important things on your plate at the moment. Next item . . .'.

Gazumped!

It's a classic story really. Good versus evil, David and Goliath, Darth Vader and Luke Skywalker. We all like to think that the forces of good always win in the end. Reality would suggest, despite Hollywood's insistence, that this is not always the case. Those who practise the black art sometimes do 'get theirs' in the end, but along the way many get hurt and rarely see justice done.

Suzanne was a consummate player of negative politics. Her methods were not overt, but they were extremely effective in eliminating the threat Martin posed to her established power base. Let's use this case study as a base for analysing the things that Martin could have done to turn this situation around.

What could Martin have done?

It is not always easy to defend yourself in the middle of a political attack. As someone once explained, 'It's like trying to change a tyre on a car travelling at 100 kilometres an hour.'

'Sleep well when the wind blows'

Success in these situations is often the result of the confidences, credibility and positive relationships developed a long time prior to the attack. Securely establishing your power base *before* attacks can take place is always the best defence.

A farmer woke one night to hear a raging and destructive wind ravaging his farm. He rushed out to the quarters

239

adjoining the homestead to find his farmhand sleeping soundly, despite the prevailing storm. He shook the sleeping farmhand violently, 'Quickly, we must secure the outer building and tether the animals.' It took the farmhand a couple of minutes to rouse himself, but after hearing the farmer's request, he rolled over and settled himself to continue his sleep.

'Get up, you dullard, and get to work quickly!' Eventually, the farmhand got up rubbing his eyes.

'No need,' he replied. 'I secure the buildings and tether the animals every night. I sleep well when the wind blows.'

In political situations like the one Martin faced, the winner is often the person who has created the most influential relationships and associations. While Martin had built a reputation for his technical competence and ability in the short time he had been with the organisation, he had not been as effective in developing alignments with those that mattered. Neither had he been as effective as he could have been in gaining insight into the political structure of the organisation or the personalities involved. He should have proactively developed these areas when he started with the company, until he gained a critical mass of support sufficient to carry him through such a situation. Ways of developing these areas and creating this 'critical mass' have been discussed earlier.

> ## Always ensure the support and ownership of those who matter before presenting an idea that makes you look good.

Know your enemy

Another error Martin made was to present his idea publicly before knowing how those involved would react. *Know your enemy.* While he was confident that his idea was viable and would be generally well received, he underestimated

Suzanne's reaction and her ability to undermine the confidence of those who mattered. He should have considered *all* of the players, identified the possible pockets of resistance and actively endeavoured to 'win them over' prior to presenting at the meeting.

Having identified his idea as a potential threat to Suzanne, Martin would have been wise to involve her in the proposal in some way or alternatively to align certain aspects of the proposal with her personal goals in order to have her 'buy in' before the meeting. If it was obvious that she was still going to object to the proposal, his next step could have been to acquire the degree of support that would constitute a critical mass. Suzanne would then have been in the minority and, consequently, a far less powerful position. This is a situation practitioners of 'the art' dislike—it would then have been likely that Suzanne would have politicked to be involved in the project, if not in charge of it.

When Martin found himself in the middle of this political storm it was really too late for him to start identifying where all of the players stood. His only option at that time was to switch into 'damage control'.

When in damage control adopt the following steps:
1. Identify who is behind the negative political activity.
2. Confront the person and find out why they are against your proposal.
3. Try to get them on side by involving them or aligning their goals with the idea.
4. Find out who else they have 'got to'.
5. Speak to each person involved to counteract any negative input.
6. Endeavour to generate as much ownership as possible and build support.
7. Cross your fingers and hope for the best.

This is by no means the 'best-case scenario'. You are much better off creating a positive political environment for yourself long before you find yourself in this situation.

241

The Seed-sowing Principle

Martin would have been well advised to have started a campaign involving the Seed-sowing Principle. This campaign would have begun a long time before his idea was implemented or suggested, and the technique used sits comfortably with those who practise positive politics— whose ultimate goal is to generate activity that benefits 'the whole' rather than 'the part'. The general concept of the idea is sown weeks, if not months, in advance and the 'seed thoughts' are allowed to germinate and grow into something that eventually bears fruit. This may include such things as:

- a casual conversation with those who might be involved
- a pertinent article, extract or book left with the right person
- a 'chance' meeting with a subject or industry expert.

Gradually, these thoughts begin to germinate, until the proposal is raised seriously, for example, at the monthly management meeting. When this occurs, it does not come as such a surprise—in fact, the comment will be, 'I was thinking along those lines myself.' The players have had the time to claim ownership of the idea. It then becomes far easier to gain support and to have the idea implemented.

Martin failed to do any of these things and, consequently, when he raised the idea at the meeting it was a surprise to all. Management had to go through the process of considering the positive and negative aspects of the suggestion and it was during this stage that Suzanne was able to undermine Martin's credibility. By 'sowing seeds' of the idea in advance, those concerned undergo the positive/negative process at their own leisure, without vested interests emphasising the negative. In fact, seed-sowing gives *you* the opportunity to emphasise the *positive*, and your proposal is given a far greater chance of acceptance.

One of the downsides of this technique is that someone else with greater influence may 'adopt' the idea as their own, stealing your thunder. For those who are not too concerned about who takes the credit or who do not have huge egos to contend with, this can be quite acceptable. If you do consider this outcome unacceptable, don't try it.

Seed-sowing is also a useful technique to use when practising 'upward management', that is, getting your boss to do the things you want them to. By using the Seed-sowing Principle skilfully, you can subtly suggest an idea until they think it is their own. Don't be surprised if one day you are called into your manager's office and told, 'Look, I've had this great idea . . .'.

Making hard decisions

It is possible that, over time, a negative political environment will become so untenable that you are being hindered from operating effectively in your job, or worse, your career has come to a grinding halt. Such a situation can call for drastic, high-risk action. At this point, you need to stop and seriously consider your main options.

Bail out

Once you realise that all stories don't have a happy ending, you may also realise that your political environment is so bad that it's time for you to cut your losses and get the hell out of there. There is a certain amount of injustice attached to this option, and you may feel a bit of a coward, but in some cases it really is the best thing to do. If your adversary has a *much* greater power base than you and has been able to secure greater respect and confidence from those in high places, the effort and time it will take for them to 'fall' or for you to exceed their lofty position may not be worth it. During this time your career could easily stagnate and your chances for opportunity, growth and development in greener fields disappear.

243

Peter

Peter worked for a high profile international organisation, having started in the ranks of lower middle management. In five years he had experienced an exceptionally rapid rise to executive management through sheer hard work, competence and confidence. He was highly regarded by the executive management team and known for his ability to get the results the company wanted—he reported directly to the Managing Director. A restructuring of the organisation saw his department amalgamated with another, and Gaye was positioned between him and the MD. Peter understood the need for the restructure and, while he was not thrilled about having to report to someone else other than the MD, accepted it as the best move for the organisation.

It was Gaye's thirst for power and control and her practice of the black arts that created Peter's problem. Any contact Peter had with executive management was 'blocked' by Gaye and the personal initiatives and 'free rein' he was able to exercise before the restructure were gradually and systematically curtailed. Peter spent two years going 'head to head' with Gaye on issues of territory and authority, making independent decisions he believed were for the good of his department, using his contacts and network for support and choosing to apologise later when it was often too late for her to intervene without losing face, to bring the tension between them to boiling point.

At the end of those two years of constant tension and confrontation, Peter stepped back and reviewed his situation. He knew that Gaye's political standing in the organisation was greater than his due to the nature of her professional expertise and the importance it held for the organisation. 'If it came to a choice between the two of us, I knew the company would have to back her. Her skill base was far more mission-critical to the success of the organisation than mine. I also knew that it was on her personal agenda to ensure I didn't progress any further in the organisation.'

In the end, Peter decided to 'bail out' in order to further his career. He chose to join a firm of management consultants, specialising in his area of expertise. 'I guess, if you look at it in terms of the power struggle, I was the one who lost. My concern was for my future career, not winning a political battle caused by someone else's insecurities. If you want to talk about winning and losing, after 18 months I was earning twice her salary. In hindsight, it was one of the best decisions of my life.'

Many people under constant political attack suffer a massive drain on their self-confidence and self-esteem. Being on the receiving end of a barrage of black art activity makes you question your competence and, at the same time, highlights your insecurities. You begin to tolerate the situation, believing it impossible that you will ever find another job. Insecurity forces people to stay in untenable work situations for far too long, when other, more viable and less stressful, opportunities and challenges are waiting.

If you review your political situation and find someone else in control of your career; if you dread going to work each day because of the tension and infighting you have to put up with; if your doctor tells you have developed an ulcer that is eating the lining out of your stomach—the answer may be risky but quite simple. Scrub up your resume and gain your revenge by giving yourself a lateral promotion out of the organisation into a better job. And then—*come back as their boss.*

Go head-to-head

This option is only for the fearless and brave at heart. In most cases, it is also for the not-so-bright. While it sounds like the kind of thing Indiana Jones would do, remember that not many of us are blessed with the dexterity and talent for getting out of danger he possessed—and he had the script before he started.

Going head to head means storming the bastions of power, openly declaring the wrongs that are being perpetrated and demanding they be righted. Set the record straight, cut them off at the knees, detail the black-art atrocities that have been going on, pull back the covers on their wily schemes—drive the stake deep into their black hearts . . . It reminds me of the final scene from too many horror movies where the hero, having fought with the villain for far too long finally triumphs, clings panting to the heroine, only for the villain to rise from the pool of blood to strike one last time. *Never* underestimate the staying power of the consummate political player. And never underestimate the damage to your career going head to head can cause if you have misread the situation or overestimated your credibility with senior management.

Try this option if you *know* the outcome before you start. Don't go into battle if you only *think* you're going to win. If you know the black art practitioner is staggering around with knives in their back already, gurgling their final breath, then this option might (possibly) be a consideration.

Fact is, this option is not good because it usually backfires. Better to live to fight another day when you are wiser and better prepared.

Boil the cauldron and cast your own spell

Having reviewed your situation you may conclude that you have nothing to lose and that you should play them at their own game.

> # WARNING! Do not try this unless accompanied by an expert.

If you are not a black art expert (chances are that you aren't if you have read this far) and decide to use the same black techniques that have been used against you—you are likely to find yourself in a dark dungeon, naked and spread-eagled on a cold, stone altar, surrounded by robed and chanting figures eager for the smell of your blood. Black art activities are not for the faint of heart or for the inexperienced. You can't just dabble in negative politics; there are no weekend warlocks. If you are unmasked as an inexperienced player, seasoned practitioners will show no mercy.

While 'going over to the dark side' may offer you a sense of achievement and sweet revenge, the chances of it backfiring are far too great. To get things done in this area you must have more power than those who oppose you. If you think you have to revert to these black techniques, you probably do so because someone has been exercising a greater source of power against you—so your chances of success are slim.

The principles of time and tide

Following Suzanne's political attack on him, Martin's best option is to start the process of rebuilding his credibility by applying the principles of 'time' and 'tide'.

'Time' is all about patience. Time has a way of fading the detail of certain events and erasing others. Martin, given time, can re-establish his standing among his management and peers and his current work will stand alone rather than in the shadow of the recent debacle. Just how long this takes can often be gauged by the weight of the circumstance, the memory of those involved and the ensuing 'good work' that follows.

'Tide' involves building a critical mass of opinion shared by a large number of people concerning your worth to the organisation. Martin must now embark upon a strategic and consistent effort focused on confirming his competence while actively seeking to develop his relationship network among his senior management and peers. His understanding of the personalities and politics at that senior level was limited and ultimately responsible for costing him the acceptance of his idea. Time should be spent gathering information and insight into the culture of the organisation—its culture, values and behavioural expectations.

Martin needs to identify the professional and personal goals of management and colleagues, so the next time he

247

needs to solicit their support he will know what 'buttons' to push. Eventually, all of this positive energy and organisational intelligence will 'turn the tide' for Martin, putting him in a better position to attempt the introduction of new ideas.

Contending with those who practise the art of negative politics is an unfortunate reality of contemporary work environments. Hopefully, in time organisations will be dominated by people who promote and practise the art of positive politics and black art practitioners will be forced to change or leave. Emerging organisational structures and enlightened management methods favour the mutually beneficial approach of those who practise positive politics. Though there will always be those who consider the black arts a viable means of achieving their personal goals, with time the effectiveness of their dark methods may diminish.

Chapter 10

THE POLITICS OF POWER AND INFLUENCE

PRINCIPLES OF USING THESE IMPORTANT TOOLS

People exercise an unconscious selection
in being influenced.

T. S. Eliot

With his brilliance, Shakespeare brought to the stage much of the cloak-and-dagger intrigue the masses suspected went on in the cold, dark corridors of power. His soliloquies gave the audience an insight into what the main players were thinking and plotting, confirming—at least in theatre—what the people had been gossiping about for years. It is no wonder that Shakespeare was such a hit with the people, and it is not surprising that his plays are still so popular today. Imagine the drama of your workplace being conducted on stage—throwing back the covers of intent and manipulation, backstabbing and poisoned motive, sharpened invective and unholy couplings. No doubt your own stories would be a sellout.

Beneath the rich, brightly hued foliage of these psychodramas lies the seedbed of the politics of power. As with Shakespeare's plays, political situations in organisations stem from the desires of individuals to gain personal advantage through establishing more effective power bases. The plotting and scheming to achieve these ends we call politics. Many people are affected along the way, and usually for the worse—one person mercilessly sacrificing another for personal gain. This is *negative politics*. Most of us hate it, and so we should.

This chapter seeks to understand 'power'—how it is used and misused in the organisational context. It looks at the role 'influence' plays in the exercise of positive politics, presenting a range of tools and techniques you can use to improve personal effectiveness in this area.

Power

'Power' is one person's ability to control the actions and behaviour of another directly, without their consent. It is the ability to utilise resources, including people, at personal discretion. There are, of course, varying degrees of power in every aspect of government, society, families and organisations and we all, in our own way, have varying levels of power. Say I enter your fruit store and demand that you hand over to me all of your money. I am obviously trying to exert power over you that I do not have. So you say 'no!'. I then take out a gun, point it at your head and reiterate my demands. Now I have power to exert force over you, to make you do as I say. The use of power here is blatant. More often, power is used in less obvious and more psychological ways.

Barton Acton said, 'Power tends to corrupt and absolute power corrupts absolutely.' He was talking about the exercise of high-level power and the tendency for people in such positions to conduct corrupt activities that negatively affect the lives of others. Such corruption occurs throughout history—Idi Amin, J. Edgar Hoover, Ferdinand Marcos, Mobutu—unfortunately the list goes on forever. There seems to be an almost irresistible temptation for humans to misuse power once it falls into their hands.

On an organisational level, the basis of organisations' operations centres around the distribution of authority, and the right and ability of individuals to utilise power at their own discretion. In an utopian environment, the distribution of power would not be a problem. Power would be used impartially to achieve the best outcome for the organisation. In reality, it doesn't work that way. The power invested in an individual is subject to a range of forces that affect the way it is used. Probably the foremost factors that determine the use of power are our personal goals and motives and the overall objectives of the organisation. But a wide variety of other forces such as the objectives of more powerful people who can influence our careers, colleagues, the people working for us, friends in the organisation, and many more are in operation.

Consequently, the distribution of power within organisations is closely linked to the exercise of politics.

The rise and rise of Ray Wilton

Ray Wilton pulled his late-model prestige car into his personally assigned car space in the executive parking area. At 44, he was the Managing Director of Systems Services for Fortron, a multinational mainframe computer manufacturer and supplier. It was 7.30 a.m. As he climbed out of his car, Lucy Shaw, one of the company's accountants, pulled her not-so-late-model, not-very-prestigious car in the carpark and parked in the spaces provided for the rank and file.

'Hey Lucy, couldn't sleep, I see.'

'Others have important work to do as well as you, Ray.'

'Tetchy. Never underestimate the importance of your bean counters, I always say.'

When Ray first headed up System Services (SS) it was regarded as the troublespot of the company. Traditionally, SS had been a source of major revenue, through the servicing of huge mainframes sold into large organisations. But with the boom in mini computers and PCs, it was becoming a department with a sunset clause. No one wanted the job, and when Ray took it on, most thought he was crazy. Ray, however, took on the business with characteristic vigour and a new creative approach. He was determined to turn the department around and make it the major revenue generator it used to be. Obviously, he could not do it through mainframes, so he began looking for other activities in which the department could become involved—ones that utilised their core skills. He was able to recreate the entire business for SS, significantly build profits and in so doing gain the attention of the worldwide organisation.

Things changed dramatically for Ray. In the early days he had found it particularly difficult to get approval for the projects he recommended. He got little co-operation from other department managers, at management meetings he hardly had a say and his input on any topic was taken very lightly. Ray was the proud owner of what others had determined was a diminishing power base. Revenues were declining, staff numbers were being cut and SS had operated in the red for over a year. Head Office accounts had actually projected the date when they expected to close his department down. This only made him more determined to turn SS around. And he did, slowly.

'I still remember the management meeting where I had put a false item on the agenda. When it came my turn to speak I ignored the topic and simply made the announcement that SS had made a profit in the last month for the first time in a year and a half. Everyone was gobsmacked. No one had noticed the figures—that was the start of the turn around for SS.'

Over the next two years Ray and his management team worked extremely hard to build the new business and to make it profitable. He called in favours, did deals, went into the field himself to convince potential clients of the worth of SS—he used every trick in the book to make SS profitable. At the same time that he built SS, Ray was (unwittingly) building his own power base. In the face of his success, Ray no longer had any trouble getting people, especially executive management, to listen to his recommendations and to grant his requests. Corporate Head Office invited him to speak at their Annual International Conference in Geneva and he developed an important network of relationships with significant people throughout the international organisation. With the success of SS, his authority and power also grew. Senior people were now seeking his advice on their personal projects. There was a scramble for other departments to get involved in joint ventures with SS.

Ray had a lot of power and he knew how to use it.

When Michael Shae poked his head into his office, Ray was genuinely pleased to see him.

'Mickey, how are you? Where you been hiding?'

'You know how it is, Ray, nose down, tail up.' Michael had worked with Ray for many years in another department at a junior level. They had been good friends.

'Got a minute, Ray? I need to talk.'

'Sure, come on in.' Michael closed the door. There was a bit of social banter and catch-up about the children.

'So tell me, Mickey, what's on your mind?'

'You have to believe this is hard for me to do. I've been thinking about talking to you for weeks.' Michael began to untangle a long and complex tale. He had been having problems at home, hired an attractive secretary because he was attracted to her, not because of her competence, they had an affair, and she then assumed some sort of privilege and power over the other staff.

'Are you still seeing her, Michael?'

'Ray, it lasted two weeks before I realised what I had done.' When he had tried to end it, the woman had threatened a sexual harassment suit. She was still causing trouble in the office and had lately started to call him at home.

'I'm starting to lose control of the situation. Ray, I need some help.'

'I assume that you are back in your right mind and that things are getting better between you and Miranda?'

'Ray, the answer is yes. The last thing I need at the moment is a "fatal attraction".'

'OK, leave it with me. Beginning next week take two weeks' holiday—just you and Miranda. Somewhere romantic where you can get your act together.'

As soon as Michael was out of the office Ray called Bob Harcourt, Human Resource Manager.

'Bob, I need a favour and some support, no questions asked.'

Ray arranged for Michael's 'problem woman' to be transferred to his own department as assistant to his secretary. For the next two weeks, while Michael was away, he worked with Bob to set her up—to demonstrate her incompetence in the new role she had accepted. Everything was done legally, to ensure they wouldn't end up with a case in the industrial relations court. Then she was fired. Just before she left, Ray took her into his office and closed the door. He never told anyone what he said to her, but neither he nor Michael heard from her again.

The bigger SS grew, the more power Ray acquired. There was a direct correlation between the size of the profit his department generated, the number of people, the resources he controlled—and the level of power he received (and, of course, the type of car he drove). For most of the time, Ray used his power base well and was highly productive, but he did use his power indiscreetly in the case of dismissing Michael's 'secretary'. Ray directly used his power in a negative way to control the outcome of some else's career.

Power in organisational terms is inextricably linked to the number of people managed and the resources controlled. The more people and resources a person directly controls, the greater the power they have. The President of the United States has access to and control of almost unlimited resources, so it is no coincidence he is referred to as the most powerful man in the world.

In an organisation where there is a scarcity of resources, any existing negative politics increases. For people to achieve their goals they need resources; where resources are not directly available, people will go out of their way to to ensure they get the most they can. This might include discrediting someone else's work, undermining confidences, telling outright lies, sabotaging a project's success—all in an effort to have better access to resources that are under someone else's direct control. In this situation, the power of those who control the resources is increased.

You can see, then, how power can easily be used to promote negative politics.

Position power

Usually the amount of formal power a person has is determined by the position they hold in an organisation and the level to which that position reports. This sort of power is generally referred to as position power—the authority that is invested in the position, not the person's inherent ability to influence others. This sort of power is usually determined by the discretionary use of resources, how much money they can spend without higher authority, the appointment of staff, the use of resources, the utilisation of their own and others' time. Position power is the type of power which can be 'wielded like a sword'. It requires no finesse, strategy or interpersonal effectiveness and there is no real compulsion to adopt a win/win/win philosophy if it does not suit. For these reasons, position power is often misused and naturally leads to the development of microcosms of negative politics. How position power is used is determined by the individual's personal goals and their feelings about other people and their personal objectives. The use of position power often ignores collaborative strategies—unless they align with the personal goals of the person holding the power.

Kurt

Kurt was the Assistant Manager Marketing for a reasonably large company that produced whitegoods. He had been with the company for almost 15 years and had seen many Marketing Directors come and go. Kurt always seemed to be the 'bridesmaid', never 'the bride', and was quietly annoyed that he was always overlooked for promotion. When Rowena Martin, the current Marketing Director resigned, executive management were caught off-guard. The company was two weeks away from launching an entire new range of product, the marketing machine was in motion and they needed someone in control to keep it on track. In desperation, and with insufficient thought, they decided that Kurt was the man for the job. Of course, Kurt was extremely positive about his appointment and knew that he was more than capable of doing the job after all these years.

On the first day in his new role Kurt got to work early and sat contentedly in his new chair, savouring the moment. It felt good. Now he would be able to do all of the things he knew the previous managers should have done. He had the power and he intended to use it.

Things started going wrong almost immediately. The first thing he did when his secretary arrived was to get her to order an entire new office suite for himself. Not that there was anything wrong with the current one, he just did not like the colour of the wood. The second thing he did was call Elizabeth Monteith into his office and inform her that if her performance did not improve, she would be terminated within the month. She had been a loyal confidante and, in his eyes, a favourite of Rowena's. This had really made him angry at the time, but there was nothing he could do about it—now he could, and he fully intended to.

Kurt continued to use his new-found power as Marketing Director indiscreetly. While Rowena had focused on the tasks at hand and sought to motivate her staff by aligning personal goals with department goals to achieve maximum productivity, Kurt played favourites without making any excuses. Roger Delahaye was appointed his new Assistant Manager—Roger also happened to be his best friend and golf partner. He had always fancied Deborah Newton, so she just happened to get some of the most important assignments while Elizabeth Monteith's gay friend, Liam, now got the most menial of tasks. The office environment changed dramatically over a short period of time, from one that was focused on clearly defined and shared organisational goals, to a cesspool of negative politics and discontent.

It took about a year before executive management began to realise that something was wrong and that they needed to take action. High staff turnover and absenteeism had not become obvious until recently and a closer examination of the department's finances revealed a tragic story. The comments made following Kurt's departure were most revealing.

'He wasn't a bad sort of guy, he just had his priorities wrong.'

'If he had only focused his attention on the job and not on the trappings that came with the job, he would have done OK.'

'With Kurt you had to always try and second guess him. What was he thinking? Where was he coming from? If you didn't say what he wanted you to say, he would ignore you.'

'Unfortunately, Kurt couldn't cope with all of the authority that came with the position. He was great as a marketeer, but hopeless when it came to handling his authority.'

Some people, when faced with the opportunity of exercising position power, let it go to their heads, allowing personal preferences free rein. As you can see with Kurt, his inability to manage the authority that came with his position caused a dramatic increase in negative politics within his team. The enduring principle that needs to be applied is—always seek a win/win/win situation.

Influence

'Influence' is a person's ability to persuade another without the use of physical or psychological force. It is the ability to get people to co-operate, share resources, lend their support and see how working together can meet personal as well as organisational goals. From this definition it is easy to see why influence is a key tool used by those who practise positive politics. Influence avoids the use of force; it is a gentle skill in practice, but an extremely potent tool in delivering outcomes. In an organisational context, those who use

257

influence as their predominant tool for achieving their objectives are not only the most successful, they are also respected and well liked by most of the people they deal with. Why? Because influence seeks to help others get what they want through the alignment of multiple objectives.

People that are adept at the practice of influence have a range of valuable qualities:

- Big picture view—they understand the broader organisational objectives and strategies
- Insight—they can clearly see the role each department will make to achieving these objectives
- Find alignment—they have the ability to identify the individual goals and to find ways of aligning these goals to achieve synergy
- Non-threatening—because they do not use force in any way they do not pose a threat or concern

People who develop and nurture these qualities will be well suited to work and succeed within the context of the emerging new organisation where there is far less emphasis on position power and a greater need to work with people across functions to achieve personal, departmental and organisational goals.

Personal power

Often people who are skilled in the use of influence are credited with having great amounts of *personal power*. As opposed to position power, personal power involves the effective use of influence to achieve a win/win/win situation. When a manager uses position power people do things because they have to, if you remember the fruit shop analogy earlier in this chapter, the shopkeeper gave up the money because there was a gun at his head. Not because he wanted to—this is a raw use of power. When a manager uses *personal power* people do things because the want to, they think it's a good idea, they can see how it will benefit them, there is mutual value to be achieved. Ultimately, personal power or influence achieves ownership among those who are important to an idea's or initiative's success.

Often those who exercise position power are threatened by those who exercise personal power, due to the fact that position power is transient and dependent on a range of variables, but personal power is a transferable skill. Position power is dependent upon a person retaining the authority bestowed upon the position they hold. This is a tenuous situation as the fortunes of organisations change so rapidly.

I worked with the director of an organisation once who wielded huge amounts of position power based upon the resources and revenue generated from his department. He held this position for a number of years, until a direction came from head office stating that the company had decided to divest itself of all non-core business. Guess what? Most of this director's department was classified non-core and, all of a sudden, he was left to manage a small and insignificant part of the business—and, all of a sudden, he had very little position power left.

A person who has built their reputation on personal power and their ability to influence others positively has developed skills they will be able to utilise continually throughout their career. Influence is an essential skill in the practice of positive politics and should be developed and utilised at every opportunity.

Irving and Cassy

Cassandra White was the Human Resource Director of an extremely large pharmaceutical organisation. She had been successful at working her way into a very senior position that retained enormous amounts of position power as well as the opportunity to affect executive-level decisions. Cassy (as she was unaffectionately referred to) was disliked by almost everyone in the organisation. In the course of her climb to the top she had trodden on and backstabbed literally hundreds of people, yet through deftness and dexterity she had avoided any major blows herself. Cassy mercilessly used her position power to pursue her personal agendas that generally centred around her accumulating more and more power to the detriment of others. As part of her strategy Cassy was building her department and seeding her people across the organisation as internal consultants to executive management. This provided her with significant control and the ability to impact any major initiative that was taking place.

A major spanner was thrown into the works when one of the executive directors started to significantly use the service of an external consultant to work in what Cassy consider to be her domain. The consultant's name was Irving Wallace-Jones. Firstly she tried to use her power base to force the executive director to stop using Irving. This resulted in a particularly vicious cat fight from which Cassy limped away to lick her wounds and rethink her strategy. She had lost this fight purely on the basis of position power—she didn't have as much as the other director did.

One of the biggest problems Cassy had was the fact that Irving, apart from being extremely effective in his role and helping to implement changes that added significant bottom line value to the organisation, was very influential. During the short time he had been working in the organisation he had made a range of good friendship at executive levels in the organisation. Irving had exceptional interpersonal skills and people genuinely liked him. He played golf with a number of executives, he was entertained by the managing director and his wife regularly and most people had only good things to say about him. Irving's influence at executive levels in the organisation was growing daily as was Cassy's frustration and anger at the way he was undermining her power and authority. There was also a certain amount of jealousy involved, for all of the years she had worked for the organisation she was still to be considered a friend by anyone in executive management, Irving seemed to be accepted with such little effort. This really annoyed her.

Cassy's second attack on Irving came in the form of

procedural irregularity. She confronted the managing director. Yes, Irving was doing an excellent job, however, he didn't seem to be responsible to anyone. We should set some parameters for his involvement and someone should monitor and control the time he spends working with us. The MD agreed that some broad parameter should be set and that Cassy should monitor the contract. She was convinced that Irving was not long for this world. She worked with the MD to set the contract and then rode Irving hard regarding fulfilment—lots of reports, feedback meetings, undue accountability, constant badgering regarding his processes and procedures. Irving managed this difficult situation well. He knew exactly what Cassy was up to and as hard as it was continued to be friendly and respectful of her position in the face of the pressure. Cassy's plans started to come unstuck when more executive managers started to request Irving's services taking him outside the parameters of the contract. She confronted the MD about this problem he said he would 'look into it'. Cassy continued to push the issue until the MD confronted her,

'Cassy, what is your problem with Irving?' she was cornered.

'What do you mean?'

'It just seems that you are hell bent on making his life difficult. You find him a threat don't you?' It was obvious the MD had hit a raw nerve ending. Cassy became nervous and jittery, she didn't reply.

'Cassy, since Irving has worked with us he has added great value to this organisation and I can see him being involved for a very long time. I will not reduce the amount of work he is doing with us simply because he threatens your sense of security. Do you understand?' Cassy nodded.

'It is not quite like that . . .'

'Look, I know exactly what it is like. Get over it!'

Cassy didn't get over it. In fact she became more obsessed with her campaign to get Irving out of the organisation. She knew that she could not use her position power to force executive management to get rid of him so she started a long term campaign to reduce Irving's effectiveness. In every situation she could use her position power to block, discredit or disrupt Irving's work, she would. It was personal now, and it was ugly.

It took almost five years, but in the end Cassy was instrumental in reducing Irving's involvement to zero. Fate played into her hands when executive managers were replaced or moved to be replaced by people who did not know Irving or were not keen to develop alliances with the associations of previous management. In the end, she got him.

Irving? He wasn't concerned at all, really. Cassy's presence made life very uncomfortable at times, but he lived with it. Irving was in great demand as a consultant. He always would be, as his influencing abilities were exceptional and could be transferred to any organisation. He also knew that ultimately Cassy would become a victim of her own power plays. Many of the enemies she had made on her journey were now meeting her at the top—it was only a matter of time.

This story illustrates the conflict that can exist between position power and personal power. In this case, position power won the day—or did it? Although it seems that perhaps Irving was the loser and Cassy the winner, it is important to see the result in long-term outcomes than in the short term. Irving, through the excellent relationships he developed with the senior executives of the organisation, actually extended his influence into other companies as they moved on. He was never going to be short of work, and he had made some good friends. Cassy, on the other hand, continued to protect and build her power base, which was actually a house of cards. If she decided to move on to another organisation there would hardly be a person who would give her a good reference, let alone someone who would employ her elsewhere. Using personal power is always superior to using position power.

The skills of influence

Influence is a skill that must be high on the list for development for those who want to be effective in the use of positive politics. Listed below are a number of skills used by those people who effectively use influence to gain political leverage:

- Communication—they can clearly express the value of co-operation in terms each individual can understand and relate to. They can also sell concepts and ideas to generate ownership and enthusiasm
- Friendliness—they have the ability to be genuinely friendly and show regard for the things that are of interest to the individual. People like them because they are focused on others rather than on themselves
- Listening—they listen to understand your point of view or concern. What is important to you is important to them
- Leverage—they can also draw on other resources they have access to, in order to help people achieve their goals. They are not selfish with their resources, they endeavour to help in any way they can
- Creativity—they are creative in finding ways to establish co-operation and the collective achievement of goals. They can create alternatives that are mutually acceptable as well as exciting
- Flexibility—while they are confident and competent in their particular line of expertise, they are also flexible enough to bend and shift to meet the needs of others
- Information—they are adept at getting people to share information that would not normally be available to them and that they need to make progress or important decision
- Interpersonal effectiveness—they like people and the challenge of achieving things through those over which they have no control. They build strong relationships and rapport with a wide range of people
- Support—they can gain the support of the people they need to achieve their goals without being in too much

263

'debt'. The value of the favours they owe do not outweigh the value received

- Upward management—they have the ability to utilise their influence skills in an upward manner just as well as they do with their peers and other team members
- Conflict management—they can negotiate conflict to ensure mutual understanding and agreement. They can turn conflict into a positive to help them achieve their goals.

Influence is the single most powerful skill you can develop to create for yourself a positive political environment. Seek it out, grow it, nurture it—and anything you wish to achieve will be within your grasp.